A Profile of the Health Management Industry

A Profile of the Health Management Industry

Health Administration for Non-Clinical Professionals

Velma Lee

A Profile of the Health Management Industry: Health Administration for Non-Clinical Professionals

First published in 2016 by
Business Expert Press, LLC
222 East 46th Street, New York, NY 10017
www.businessexpertpress.com

ISBN-13: 978-1-60649-982-5 (paperback)
ISBN-13: 978-1-60649-983-2 (e-book)

Business Expert Press Industry Profiles Collection

Collection ISSN: 2331-0065 (print)
Collection ISSN: 2331-0073 (electronic)

Cover and interior design by S4Carlisle Publishing Services Private Ltd., Chennai, India

First edition: 2016

10 9 8 7 6 5 4 3 2 1

Printed in the United States of America.

Abstract

The World Health Organization's (WHO) constitution states that its objective "is the attainment by all people of the highest possible level of health" (World Health Organization, Constitution of the World Health Organization (PDF), p.1. Accessed 11 November 2013), which includes directing authorities in health policy and work, supplying technical assistance to governments on request during emergencies, and coordinating with the United Nations, governmental health administrations, specialized agencies, and professional groups for effective collaboration. According to the U.S. Census Bureau, a significant component of the healthcare industry in the country comprises establishments with physicians and other medical staff engaged primarily in providing a range of outpatient medical services to health maintenance organization (HMO) subscribers, with focus on primary health care. These establishments are owned by the HMO. Included in this industry are HMOs that both provide healthcare services and underwrite health and medical insurance policies (NCAIS code 621491 refers to HMO medical centers).

Health practitioners or health practitioner groups contracting to provide services to subscribers of prepaid health plans are classified under Industry 62111, Offices of Physicians; Industry 621210, Offices of Dentists; and Industry Group 6213, Offices of Other Health Practitioners. HMOs (except those providing healthcare services) engaged primarily in underwriting and administering health and medical insurance policies are classified under Industry 524114, Direct Health and Medical Insurance Carriers. What will not be discussed in this book are other healthcare approaches, including commercial, welfare, patient, Medicare, employer-direct contracting, and privately paid (i.e., cash-based traditional, chiropractic, naturopathic, etc.)

Health care is traditionally viewed as a science profession, with a public service focus, it now includes major partnering organizations, including the insurance industry, the pharmaceutical industry, academic research centers, various specialization groups, laboratory agencies, social workers, and supermarket chains. Hospitals exist in many organizational forms and structures—sole-proprietary clinics, government-funded hospitals, franchised groups, and hybrids that offer both publicly and privately funded services.

Over the last two decades, there are increased offerings of Masters in Health Care Administration degrees offered in various shades and depths by higher educational institutions. Yet, it is difficult to find one text that serves as a central platform for any instructor to build a course upon. Most of the course materials of such a graduate degree come from a variety of reading materials determined by the teaching instructors' expertise and resources.

This book is intended for middle- and upper-level managers in healthcare organizations who have no or little clinical training background. Students of healthcare administration and those who would like to enter the field may find it useful.

Keywords

administration, competition, electronic medical record, ethics, healthcare, healthcare leadership, healthcare policy, HMO, human resources, insurance, management, medical centers, strategy

Contents

Foreward

Whether you are a student considering the health care profession, planning to join the industry as a mid-career seasoned manager, or simply an ordinary citizen whose dear family/ friend needs medical treatment, you will find this book useful in giving you information and perspective about the health care industry to ask the right questions.

—Arturo BLANCO, M.D.

Purpose

A significant component of healthcare industry comprises establishments with physicians and other medical staff engaged primarily in providing a range of outpatient medical services to health maintenance organization (HMO) subscribers, with focus on primary health care (NCAIS code 621491 refers to HMO Medical Centers). The healthcare industry also includes insurance, pharmaceuticals, ambulatory services, rehabilitation, and hospitality. This book provides an overview of the industry to nonclinical practitioners to understand selected historical milestones and trends that are significant to healthcare leadership and management.

Pertinent legislations and the industry landscape are changing almost on a daily basis. It is not the intent of this book to provide the readers with most updated trends and information of the field. Rather, it serves as background knowledge and provides some basis for which management new to the healthcare industry can begin asking relevant questions and more in-depth discussions with regard to one's entity or peripheral industry.

Acknowledgments

This book is not possible without the support and encouragement of many—first and foremost, my husband and daughter. I also want to thank my husband's family and relatives, my parents' training of my thirst for knowledge and filling gaps where needed, many colleagues and students at Palm Beach Atlantic University and students who helped research and contribute to this piece of work, as well as friends and family in the medical field in California, New York, Florida, Texas, and Washington.

My mentors in the United Kingdom, United States, and Hong Kong who have researched and published in the healthcare industry and practitioners in the field who have offered me their views and reflection over the years have all contributed to the birth of this piece of work.

I am also much indebted to the Business Expert Press team's editorial support, especially Rene Caroline.

Overview

Chapter 1 offers an overview of the basic elements in a healthcare institution from an organizational perspective. It discusses human resources, core departmental functions, financing, and future challenges.

The healthcare industry is rich in history and development. It has experienced many periods of change and growth. To understand how the industry operates, Chapter 2 briefs some historical landmarks, paradigm shift, and changes in physical building code requirements. Legislative requirements and changing regulations' impact on relevant constituents highlighted the complex and competitive nature of the industry.

Chapter 3 focuses on health care as a hybrid product and service commodity. Health care is analyzed from a marketing perspective. It also highlights changes in demographics, impact of technological advancement, shifting societal values, and patient expectations. This chapter concludes with more elaboration on common human resources issues and challenges. Some data and trends are presented but readers should update their knowledge using the data source provided to get the latest information regarding the industry landscape.

Chapter 4 continues a discussion on competitive strategy regarding pricing, entry barriers, different funding sources, strategic stakeholders, and strategic alliances.

Chapter 5 discusses governmental regulations as it has major influence on healthcare policies. Of primary concern are policies that promote or restrict access to health care and quality of service rendered both in the short- (e.g., patient experience) and long-term (e.g., overall wellness, recovery rate with no development of other illness, etc.). Patient and employee safety are highly regulated through AMA, OSHA, food safety laws with nutritionist guidelines, HIPAA, medical ethics committees, and requirements for accommodations for patients with disabilities and no insurance coverage. As a labor-intensive industry, unions, governmental wage/labor regulations, and market competition influence service quality and profitability. Globalization and medical tourism is spurring more financial and legal implications that require regulations, ethical practices, and investment in more efficient and effective healthcare delivery. Sustainability as well as other opportunities and challenges are also discussed.

CHAPTER 1

Elements of Health Care

In this section, we summarize typical organizational structures found in the health care industry, functions of various departments, and market- versus government-based financing.

Human Resources

According to the World Health Organization (WHO), human capital decisions include an appropriate quality, mix, and distribution of health services. To find the right balance, careful choices made by countries in light of their unique needs, and monitoring, are important. At the organizational level, human resources planning is a crucial function that is often neglected.[1] To forecast supply and demand of human resources in hospitals, one must understand typical organizational structures in the industry.

Typical Organizational Charts

In this section, three types of organizational structures are described, though there are many other types and sizes of hospitals that exist in the U.S. system. Veteran Administration (VA) hospitals are 100 percent government funded, and are not covered in this book. This does not mean that they represent a minority, or are less significant. However, management, financing, and accountability of a VA hospital are very different from a private, community, or emerging hybrid form of healthcare institution; so it is fair only if a more thorough, separate discussion is devoted to the subject.

[1]Fred C. Lunenberg, "Human Resource Planning: Forecasting Demand and Supply," *International Journal of Management Business, and Administration* 15, no. 1 (2012): 1.

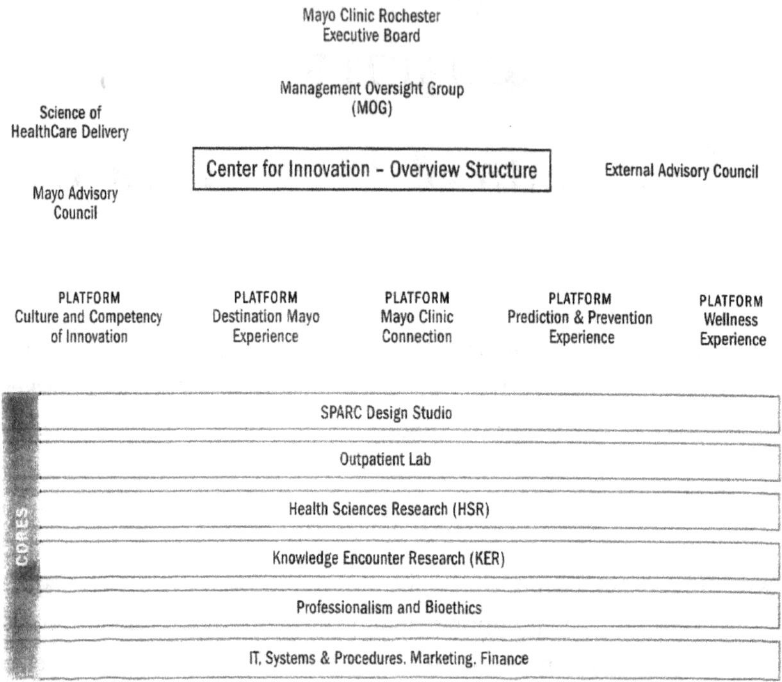

Figure 1.1 Organizational Chart of Mayo Clinic

Source: Smith, A.N. (2010, November 23). CFI Structure. *Yale School of Management*. (2010). Retrieved from http://nexus.som.yale.edu/design-mayo/?q=node/114

Research Hospital (e.g., Mayo Clinic)

The objective of a research-focused healthcare institution is to provide patients with the latest and best treatments for advanced diseases that general hospitals do not have the resources to treat. Patients are aware that the treatments they receive might be part of larger research that involves undocumented risks.

Figure 1.1 shows the organizational chart of the Mayo Clinic. The Mayo Clinic was founded by Dr. William Worrall Mayo in 1864, with a medical school opened in 1972. It was the world's first private, integrated, group medical practice, where patient care and teamwork were the center of medical practice.[2] During the 1980s, the Mayo Clinic opened in Jacksonville, Florida. In the 1990s, the clinic's first website was created,

[2]"Mayo Clinic History," History of Mayo Clinic, accessed May 20, 2015, http://www.mayoclinic.org/about-mayo-clinic/history.

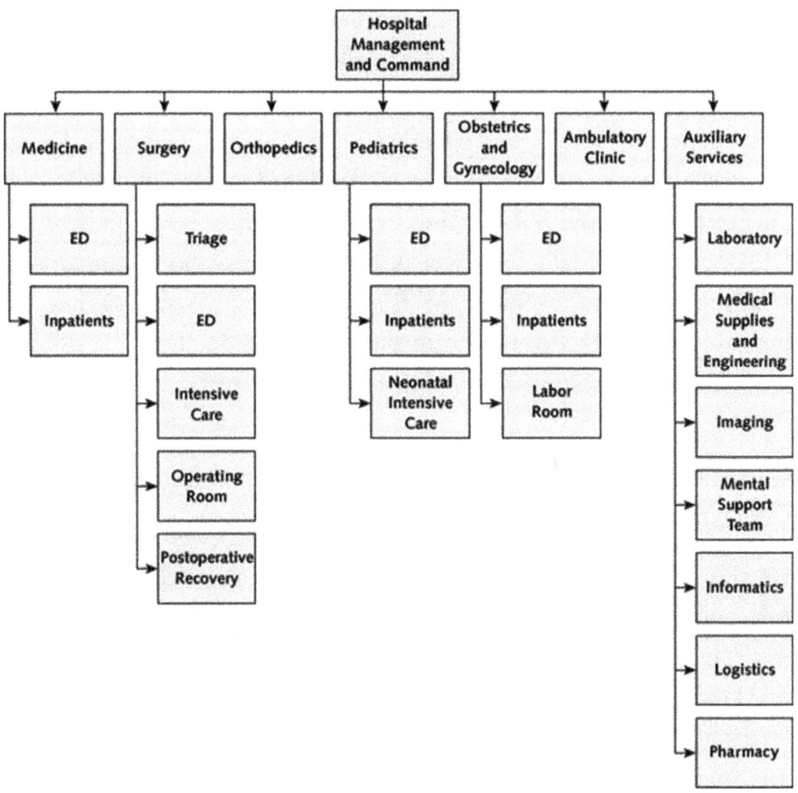

Chart 1.2 A typical hospital organizational chart

Chart 1.2 shows a typical hospital's organizational chart, depicting departments that are common concern for staffing and management.

and the children's hospital opened. In 2001, scientists at Mayo developed the first rapid anthrax diagnoses following the 9/11 terrorist attack. In 2010, Mayo launched "decade to discovery," with the purpose of curing both Type I and Type II diabetes by 2020. In 2013, legislation was passed to approve public funding for Destination Medical Center, which is expected to be a $6 billion investment over a 20-year period.[3]

Private Institutions (e.g., Virginia Mason Medical Center and Hospital)

Virginia Mason Medical Center (VMMC) is a private, nonprofit hospital. Its funding comes from private sources, and it is not responsible to the

[3]Ibid.

government. It embodies a typical hospital organizational structure, and more. For example, it has a special quality assurance department called the Kaizen Promotion (KP) office which focuses on hospital efficiency while delivering world-class patient service. The Administrative Director of KP, together with the Senior VP for Quality and Compliance, report to the Executive VP of Chief Operating Officer (COO). Both the COO and Chief Medical Officer (CMO) report to the Chairman and CEO. VMMC's management goal is to equip frontline staff, so they can improve daily work and transform the way things are done.[4] It also has specialization of treatment for AIDS and plastic surgery.

Current Hybrid (e.g., University of Southern California Healthcare Center)

University of Southern California Healthcare Center (USC HCC) is a representative of the development of many university research-based hospitals, which evolved from a pure research/teaching institute to one that provides premises for teaching physicians to accept patients on a private level while continuing research and teaching. This hybrid form of healthcare organization usually has two organizational charts. 1. A research-based organizational chart that shows the areas of services and expertise. 2. A revenue-generating, private healthcare center that look like a for-profit organization, with slightly different compensation and benefits systems.

Similarities and Differences

Although all three types of organizational structures have similar missions, functions, and service mottos, their sources of financing and dependence on state budgets versus private patients with independent governance provide different degrees of incentives and flexibility for planning, training, and retention of human resources. For example, USC was originally affiliated with the university, and all staff benefits operated like the rest of other academic departments in the university. Over time, the hospital had different sections that were privatized, and organizations such as Tenet

[4]Joanne Conroy et al., "Virginia Mason Medical Center: Applying LEAN Methodology to Lead Quality and Transform Health," *AAMC Readiness for Reform* (2011): 5–8.

Healthcare Corporation took control and started giving it new name, logo, regulations, and so on. Although the outside of the healthcare facility might not present notable difference to the average patient, the internal policies and difference in staff compensation system (dependent on their joining era as a university staff or a private hospital organization staff) can be distinct. When two types of differently compensated healthcare professionals work in parallel, there are potential conflicts regarding objectives, speed, and quality focus. There might also be duplication of duties and positions for a significant transition period prior to clarification of new roles and responsibilities.

Divisions

Outpatient service/treatment (OS/T) refers to treatment of patients who do not require hospitalization. There is also increased emphasis on care for those who have been released recently from the hospital or were admitted to the hospital for overnight monitoring. OS/T has been gaining importance over the years since hospital performance is now monitored more closely and hospitalization expenses skyrocketed. There have been increased pushes to discharge patients from the hospital earlier so their care can be provided in the least expensive way that still accords with positive medical outcomes. Many hospital affiliated urgent care centers are established in the last two decades. According to research of the United States Department of Labor, consumer prices for outpatient healthcare services increased 200 percent from 1997–2015. Over the same period, there was an overall 50 percent increase of all items. Medicare/insurance companies have strict criteria and definitions for technically admitting patients into the hospital. OS/T plays a role in determining how patients are treated and whether they are considered outpatient/hospitalized patients from a billing perspective. Many healthcare organizations choose to strengthen support offered by OS/T to boost overall patient satisfaction and lower cost. Below are elaborations on a few divisions that complement OS/T.

Medical Records and Patient History

Medical records are increasingly organized in electronic health systems, which offer convenient storage and retrieval. However, medical records also create high risk of fraud and identity theft once information is available to unethical groups. For patient safety and privacy concerns, patients must fill out an "Authorization for Release of Information" form to receive medical records before being discharged/picked up.[5] The U.S. Government has aggressively pushed medical organizations to adopt electronic medical records systems, offering financial incentives for implementation and imposing penalties for failure to timely achieve these goals. Good record keeping allows for better medical diagnosis and treatment, potentially resulting in fewer readmission of patients to hospitals. The average service budget for this area is about 4 percent of annual total operational cost.[6] Reliable maintenance of computer servers and storage backups are important challenges for this department. "What are ways to protect patient information while maintaining the application of advanced technology for improved communication and consistent medical care?" is a question worthy of strategic concern and management attention.

Diagnostic Services

Diagnostic services facilitate the provision of timely, cost-effective, high-quality diagnostic care in secure environments.[7] Pathology, laboratory medicine, radiology, and nuclear medicine are components of diagnostic services. Correct diagnoses are important for the right treatment and patient recovery. Most diagnostic blood tests can be completed with simple chemical procedures and minimal laboratory time. Diagnostic tests such as blood tests are typically less expensive. However, radiology- and cardiology-related diagnostic tests, and cancer genetic diagnostic tests, are more complicated and expensive. Acquisition costs of radiology equipment are high, but tests can be run inexpensively after the equipment is obtained.[8] Some tests cost minimally while others are expensive, depending on whether a physician's

[5]"Patients and Visitors," Baylor Health Care System, accessed March 4, 2014, www.baylorhealth.com/PatientVisitors/Pages?MedicalRecords.aspx.

[6]Take average from Washington State Department of Health, 2013; Red River Hospital, 2014.

[7]"Patient Care Services: Diagnostic Services," US Department of Veterans Affairs, accessed March 4, 2014, www.patientcare.va.gov/DiagnosticsServices.aspx.

[8]David Belok, "The True Cost of Healthcare," accessed December 15, 2011, http://truecostofhealthcare.org/outpatient_charges/diagnostic_tests.

interpretation is required. The average budget for this department is about 5 percent of annal total operational cost.[9]

Pharmacy

The traditional role of pharmacist has transformed from that of a dispenser of medications to that of a vital healthcare team member who consults closely with patients with chronic diseases, offers medication adherence strategies, and broadens the profession's overall influence.[10] For example, during management of insulin levels for diabetic patients, pharmacists help with both tests and glucose monitoring, which is expected to reduce death rates from 75 percent to 45 percent in 100,000.[11] Over $100 billion was spent in 2011 just on diabetic-related pharmaceuticals and supplies,[12] and these expenses are expected to increase in the years to come. Some medications can be addictive, so there is the ethical dilemma of prescribing medications to patients that are not supposed to make them more drug-dependent. Another area of debate is the use of generic versus new drugs. Medicare has a policy on restricted adoption of new drugs. Generic drugs are usually affordable, whereas new drugs (e.g., a drug that treats Hepatitis C in 90 days but costs thousands of dollars) are much more expensive. Average hospital budget for a pharmacy department is about 7 percent of annal total operational cost.[13]

---

[9]Take average from Washington State Department of Health, 2013; Red River Hospital, 2014.

[10]Bea Riemschneider, "The Next-Generation Pharmacist: What Will the Future Look Like for Pharmacy?" *Pharmacy Times*, last modified September 28, 2010, accessed March 14, 2014, www.pharmacytimes.com/publications/issue/2010/September2010/NGP_Future_of_Pharmacy-0910.

[11]Victoria J. Babb and John Babb, "Pharmacist Involvement in Healthy People 2010," American Pharmaceutical Association, last modified 2003, accessed March 14, 2014, http://pharmacy.auburn.edu/pcs/mtms/Pharmacistinvolvementinhealthypeople2010.pdf.

[12]Lisa A. Davis, "Acute Care Hospital Expenses for FY 2011," Connecticut Department of Public Health, last modified February 2013, accessed March 14, 2014, www.ct.gov/dph/lib/dph/ohca/publications/2013/2011_expense_fact_sheet.pdf.

[13]Taking an average from Massachusetts Hospital Association, 2012; Washington State Department of Health, 2013; Virginia Mason Medical Center, 2014.

Anesthesia

Anesthesia is an indispensable part of surgery. The various types of anesthesia include local, regional, spinal, and epidural, and general. The medical definition of anesthesia is the "loss of feeling in a person's body or part of the body through the use of drugs."[14] Although anesthesia is used commonly in everyday surgery, there is a small but real risk of injury. The largest risk relates to the underlying medical/surgical conditions of the patient, and the procedure being performed. There is additional risk based on a patient's unique response to medication, and a correspondingly higher adverse outcome due to improper administration.[15] Due to the acute nature of surgery and higher risk for more adverse outcomes, medical malpractice and negligence lawsuits are common in this department. Having protection from potential legal disputes for both physicians and hospitals is important. The average budget for this department is about 7 percent of annal total operational cost.[16]

Diet and Nutrition

Diet and nutrition services in hospitals strive to provide quality food and nutrition during both inpatient and outpatient services. Inpatient nutrition services include an interdisciplinary care team that monitors medical nutrition therapy and ensures each patient has a nutrition plan specified to individual needs.[17] Outpatient dietitians often deal with patients seeking help with diabetes, high cholesterol, weight loss, hypertension, kidney disease, and cancer. Hospital dietitians play a role in the health and recovery of patients (e.g., after surgery) who have special dietary and nutritional needs. It also forms part of the hospitality division that contributes

---

[14]"Anesthesia," *Merriam-Webster*, accessed March 15, 2014, www.merriam-webster.com/dictionary/anesthesia.

[15]Henry K. Beecher and Donald P. Todd, "A Study of the Deaths Associated with Anesthesia and Surgery: Based on a Study of 599,548 Anesthesias in Ten Institutions 1948–1952, Inclusive," *Annals of Surgery* 140, no. 1 (1954): 2.

[16]Taking an average from Baylor Health, 2010; Washington State Department of Health, 2013; Virginia Mason Medical Center, 2011.

[17]Washington State Department of Health, "Nutrition and Food Services", 2014.

to patient experiences. Options are sometimes multiple. For example, if a diabetic patient had a stroke and cannot swallow, a dietitian must make recommendations to the physician regarding the proper feeding tube formula, and monitor the patient's nutritional status. Dietary services represent 30 percent of an average hospital's budget.[18]

Specialty Referral

When a primary physician refers a patient to a specialist, it is believed that the specialist is more qualified concerning diagnosis and treatment.[19] Physicians also minimize malpractice risk by referring patients to specialists. The patient will likely receive more tests and have higher costs than if cared for by the original, primary-care physician. The advantage lies in receiving the help of a trusted physician trained in the area the patient needs the most. This department comprises approximately 11 percent of a hospital's annual budget.[20] Major challenges in this department include budget cuts and competition from increasing networks of specialists.

Rehabilitation

Rehabilitation has the potential to improve both physical functioning and overall longevity in older patients. A challenge that inpatient rehabilitation hospitals encounter is increasing numbers of nursing homes' capability of performing stabilization of an original medical complication, causing patient loss. Some suggests that inpatient rehabilitation hospitals average longer lifespans for patients in comparison to nursing homes, making the former the preferred form of treatment center. It is likely that those who go through rehabilitation have more discipline to recover

---

[18]Taking an average from Food Labor Budget, 2004; Washington State Department of Health, 2013.

[19]Christopher B. Forrest et al., "Primary Care Physician Specialty Referral Decision Making: Patient, Physician, and Health Care System Determinants," John Hopkins University, last modified September 09, 2010, accessed May 18, 2014, www.jhsph.edu/research/centers-and-institutes/johns-hopkins-primary-carae-policy-center/Publications_PDFs/A216.pdf.

[20]Taking an average from Massachusetts Hospital Association, 2012; Baylor Health, 2010.

and family support while those in nursing homes may be left with less supervision and accountability to recover for the long run. Apart from the medical needs of the patient, insurance availability is sometimes the determinant for patient rehabilitation in a nursing home or a rehabilitation center. The rehabilitation department makes up approximately 20 percent of the average hospital's annual bud.[21]

Spiritual Option

Spirituality is offered in numerous ways across hospitals. Spiritual services may include a chaplain's visit, daily service in a chapel, blessings of newborn babies, advice on funeral choices, and help with ethical healthcare decisions. Many hospitals also have programs that aid with bereavement and the loss of a family member. Palliative care is the current paradigm regarding treating near-death patients. The quality of life (as affected by the complexity of many other existing illnesses/absence of a supportive family community/seniority in age) of a patient with a terminal disease is considered heavy during decisions of treatment concerning prolonging life. Spiritual services make up about 7 percent of the average hospital's budget.[22] With shifting focus from a "care" to "cure" model, complemented by use of technology, it is becoming increasingly challenging to balance spirituality (let a patient die naturally to return to heaven/earth) and the use of technology for prolonging life (with the possibility of lowered quality of life for the patient).

Financing and Insurance

The days have passed since the government was the major source of funding for public hospitals. In 2014, the University of California at Los Angeles (UCLA) Medical Center received 3 percent of its funding from the state.[23]

---

[21] Taking an average from Virginia Mason Medical Center, 2014; Health Glossary, 2013.

[22]Taking an average of Massachusetts Hospital Association, 2012 and Virginia Mason Medical Center, 2014.

[23]Reed Hutchinson, "CFO Explains Hospital's Finance to Employees," *UCLA Today: Faculty and Staff News*, accessed April 28, 2014, www.today.ucla.edu/portal/ut/PRN-050816people_cfo.aspx.

According to the 2014 *California State Auditor*, more than 95 percent of the total revenue generated by each medical center came from patient service provision.[24] Patient revenue generated more than three times of UCLA Medical Center's income in 2014, in comparison to non-patient revenue.[25] Non-patient funds usually include grants, contributions, tax support, and miscellaneous income. Virginia Mason Medical Center generates income by issuing corporate bonds. In 2013, it issued $136M of new, 30-year taxable corporate bonds.[26] Baylor University Medical Center receives revenue from direct and indirect public support, government grants, interest on cash investments, and dividends and interest from securities.[27] Trends show that hospitals are increasingly investing more in stock markets since payments from private and government insurers are shrinking.[28]

Most hospitals invest in many types of insurance for protection against liability. Examples include director and officers' liability insurance, employment practices liability insurance, errors and omissions insurance, equipment breakdown insurance, and commercial general liability. All of these insurances are designed to protect the hospital in case of lawsuit, error, or malpractice.

Insurance companies also understand the relationship between quality and cost, and know the value of promoting good outcomes. Thus, they encourage hospitals to reduce malpractice insurance by documenting data that can demonstrate risk reduction. For example, if a hospital can show that it meets the National Patient Safety Goals established by the Joint

---

[24]Elaine M. Howle, "UCLA and UCSF Medical Centers," *California State Auditor: Fact Sheet* (2014): 1.

[25]"Identification and Characteristics: Ronald Reagan UCLA Medical Center," American Hospital Directory, accessed April 26, 2014, www.ahd.come/free_profile.php?-hcfa_id=a5ba61dcb726a71c1e7cb701b5b1ac1e&ek=6f44eb5cdeb9df9bd112040a543697a2.

[26]Charles Margolis, "Virginia Mason Medical Center's New 30-yr Taxable Bond," *Learn Bonds*, last updated 2013, accessed April 26, 2014, www.learnbonds.com/-virginia-mason-medical-centers-news-30-year-taxable-bonds.

[27]FAQS, "Baylor University Medical Center in Dallas, Texas (TX)," accessed April 27, 2014, www.faqs.org/tax-exempt/TX/Baylor-University-Medical-Center.html.

[28]Andrew L. Wang, "How Chicago's Top Hospitals Really Make Money," *Chicago Business*, accessed February 3, 2014, www.chicagobusiness.com/article/20140201/-ISSUE01/302019986/how-chicagos-top-hospitals-really-make-money.

Commission, it is awarded points. If a hospital exceeds the national average by 5 percent, it is awarded additional points. Points accumulated can be translated to premium credits, where the hospital is charged a lower premium, possibly saving millions of dollars. Such savings are sizable, and administrators are learning to incorporate quality variables in financial reports.[29] Other variables insurance companies consider to encourage hospitals to improve quality of care include length of stay, readmission rate, etc.

Health Insurance Costs in Private Industry

According to the Bureau of Labor Statistics, in In March 2015, the average cost of health insurance benefits was $2.43 per hour worked in private industry (7.7 percent of total compensation). Among occupational groups, employer costs for health insurance benefits ranged from $0.89 per hour worked and 6.1 percent of total compensation for service workers to $3.71 and 6.6 percent of total compensation for management, professional, and related occupations. Among other occupational categories, employer costs for health benefits averaged $2.09 (8.7 percent of total compensation) for sales and office occupation, lower than $2.90 (8.5 percent) for natural resources, construction, and maintenance occupations, and $2.74 (10.1 percent) for production, transportation, and material moving occupations. Employer costs for health insurance benefits were higher for union workers, averaging $5.65 per hour worked (12.1 percent of total compensation), than for non-union workers, averaging $2.11 (7 percent). In goods-producing industries, health insurance benefit costs were higher, at $3.30 per hour worked (8.9 percent of total compensation), than in service-providing industries, at $2.25 (7.4 percent).[30]

Key Terms Definition and Distinction

1. Health maintenance organizations (HMO) provide individuals and families enrolled voluntarily in a geographic area with comprehensive

[29]Yosef D. Dlugacz, *Value-Based Health Care: Linking Finance and Quality* (San Francisco: Jossey-Bass Publishing, 2010), 76–77.

[30]"Economic News Release," Bureau of Labor Statistics, last modified December 9, 2015, accessed June 10, 2015, www.bls.gov/news.release/ecec.nr0.htm.

health care through member physicians. They are usually financed by fixed, periodic payments determined in advance with limited referrals to outside specialists.

2. A PPO, a preferred provider organization, gives consumers of healthcare contracts economic incentives to patronize one's preferred physician, laboratory, and hospital, who agrees to reduced fees and supervision.
3. Established in the 1960s, Medicare is a government program of medical care designed for the elderly. Medicaid is a program of medical aid for those unable to afford regular medical service. It is managed by the state, but financed jointly by the state and federal government.
4. Managed care is a system of providing health care to patients who agree to limited selection regarding the choice of physician. It achieves cost containment through managed programs in which a physician accepts restrictions on the amount charged for medical care. Medical homes are also known as patient-centered medical homes. They consist of team-based healthcare delivery, led by a physician who provides comprehensive and continuous medical care to patients with the goal of obtaining maximized health outcomes.

Financing Models

Generally, a hospital's major categories of expenses include employee salaries, equipment purchases and maintenance, service contractors, consumable supplies, and repayments on bank loans. Apart from non-patient income such as treasury bonds, trustee donations, and other miscellaneous sources of funding, typical financing comes from serving the health and medical needs of a community. Patients pay for services directly out-of-pocket, through government programs such as Medicaid and Medicare, or through insurance companies, private employers, and others. In the United States, a challenge lies in that healthcare institutions depend heavily on a limited number of paying clients for most of their operating funding. The largest customers are often the federal or state governments. Dealing with government entities involves a substantial amount of reporting to ensure compliance and adherence to regulations. For hospitals to be reimbursed, it also involves deep knowledge of complicated and longitudinal calculation methods since the system changes across generations. For example, calculation of payments to a hospital under Medicare inpatient services involves four elements: prospective payments, DRG operating payment, DRG capital payment,[31] and reasonable cost of payments.[32] These payments might increase from indirect medical education (for teaching hospitals), disproportionate share (hospitals that treat a large portion of Medicaid- and Medicaid-eligible patients), and outlier payments (patients who use an unusually large amount of resources). All involve knowledge of the computations to secure payment.

There are also numerous payment systems regarding hospitals/physicians that involve disparate payment units. The four major ones are historical cost reimbursement (reasonable cost and apportionment), specific services (charge payment, a discount from the master price list), capitated rates (cost of service and utilization balance needed), and bundled services (hospitals paid by some healthcare plans per diem or case payment rate). The field is constantly changing. For instance, Medicare proposed to start paying hospitals fixed amounts for hip and knee replacements, rather than letting providers bill individually for each surgical and recovery service provided to older Americans in July 2015.[33] An estimated $150 million will be saved over five years from 2016 onwards. For details, one should keep abreast of the evolving regulatory changes. Cleverley and Song (2011) has a book titled "Essentials of Health Care Finance" which is also a great reference for those interested in this area.

For Medicare outpatient service, the Balanced Budget Act of 1997 directed implementation of a prospective payment system (PPS). All

---

[31]DRG system is developed by Yale University, which takes all possible diagnoses from the *International Classification of Diseases, 9th revision, Clinical Modification (ICD-9-CM)* system and classifies them into 25 major diagnostic categories based on the organ systems. These 25 categories are further broken down into distinct medically meaningful groups or DRGs. It is expected that resources needed to treat a disease within a DRG category should be similar for all patients. The number of DRGs have increased significantly over time to over 750.

[32]Williams O. Cleverley and Paula H. Song, *Essentials of Health Care Finance*, 7th ed. (Sudbury: Jones & Bartlett Learning, 2011), 42.

[33]Louise Radnofsky and Stephanie Armour, "Medicare Plans Fixed Rate on Knee, Hip Replacements," *The Wall Street Journal* A4 (July 10, 2015).

services paid under the new PPS are classified into groups called ambulatory payment classifications (APCs). Services in each APC are similar in clinical and resource requirements. The Act also changed the way beneficiary coinsurance is determined.[34]

In summary, one needs to have good understanding of both the organizational culture and political environment of the healthcare entity one serves (whether it is skilled nursing facility, home health agency, and so on), and be knowledgeable about its payment computation system (e.g., resource utilization groups III and elements for adjustment) to ask questions that may lead to innovation and begin to improve the financing model.

Current Controversy

The question of favorable patient selection—the contention that specialty hospitals treat a more financially favorable selection of patients in comparison to general hospitals—has added to the debate about the advantages and drawbacks of specialty hospitals. This issue links with the way hospitals are paid. The fixed-rate, lump-sum payments that Medicare and many other healthcare payers typically make to hospitals for inpatient care for patients with a given diagnosis, regardless of the costs of serving particular patients, are designed to promote efficiency by discouraging hospitals from providing unnecessary services to boost revenues. However, these lump sum payments foster undesirable incentives since hospitals might gain financially by serving a disproportionate share of lower-cost patients with the same diagnoses. Medicare's hospital payment system rules illustrate this principle.

Under its system of prospective payments, Medicare pays a predetermined rate for each hospital discharge, based on the patient's diagnosis and whether the patient received surgery. Payments reflect an average bundle of services that the beneficiary is expected to receive as an inpatient for a diagnosis. Discharges are classified according to a list of DRGs. DRG payment rates are based on the expected cost of the diagnosis group's typical case in comparison to the cost for all Medicare inpatient cases. The DRG payment is not adjusted for within-DRG differences regarding severity of illness. Therefore, hospitals have a financial incentive to treat

[34]For detail example and calculation, refer to Cleverley and Song, *Essentials of Health Care Finance*, 33–51.

as many patients as possible whose costs are low relative to the costs of the average patient in each DRG.[35] One of the issues with DRG is that it can be legally upcoded to increase the billing price for treatments according to a hospital's service to the community. In some medical "charity" facilities,[36] where a huge portion of uninsured patients are treated, the federal government allows a hospital to upcode selected DRGs, making other patients pay more to compensate for the uninsured.

Beginning in 2015, the coding system ICD-10 was enforced. It is the 10th revision of the international statistical classification of disease and related health problems (ICD), a medical classification list by the World Health Organization. It contains very specific codes for disease, symptoms, issues, social circumstances and causes of problem, etc. ICD-10 is a very sophisticated and specific system, making implementation even more challenging for many hospitals.

Regarding charity hospitals, some cities and states require citizens to help fund the operations via taxes based on property ownership and location. For instance, in the city of Dallas, Texas, where the uninsured population is huge, homeowners are required to pay tax to help fund charity hospitals.[37]

In the late 1980s, lawmakers required hospitals to treat patients regardless of their insurance and citizenship status. As a result, about $2 billion per year has been funded for emergency treatment for a group of patients who, according to most hospitals, are mostly illegal immigrants with a small percentage of homeless and new immigrants. Some criticized the availability of such services, which encouraged more people to cross the border illegally.[38] According to an interview with the chief financial officer of Bethesda Healthcare System in Boynton Beach of Florida—one that treats many new and illegal immigrants, the hospital staff could not

---

[35]"Geographic Location, Services Provided, and Financial Performance," The General Accounting Office, last Modified October 2003, accessed April 28, 2014, http://gao.gov/new.items/d04167.pdf.

[36]From a practitioner's perspective, some hospitals are called medical "charity" hospitals.

[37]Phillip Galewitz, "Medicaid Helps Hospitals Pay for Illegal Immigrants' Care," last modified February 12, 2013, accessed April 28, 2014, http://khn.org/news/medicaid-illegal-immigrant-emergency-care/.

[38]Ibid.

turn the patients away because of its proximity to the farms where many harvest sugarcane and seasonal produces.[39] New York, North Carolina, Florida, Texas, Arizona, and Illinois are all states that spent millions of dollars on Emergency Medicaid to treat thousands of people annually.[40]

Prior to the enactment of the Affordable Care Act (ACA; 2014), states had approximately 30 percent of uninsured citizens in the healthcare system. Who treats patients who cannot afford the regular cost of health services and medicine when they needed? Many answers are possible, but the majority of poor people in the system might end up in medical facilities where medical students (intern residents who might be paid one-third the market rate) who are learning medicine treat them under the supervision of a physician professor. Examples of these healthcare facilities include Harborview Medical Center (WA), Harbor UCLA Medical Center (CA), and Parkland and Ben Taub Hospitals (TX). This type of hospitals has unique positions concerning billing Medicare patients due to the disproportionally higher volume of uninsured people treated. More elaboration is made under the DRG section.

ACA, also known as Obamacare, which requires all Americans to be covered by health insurance, is one of the most contested mandates in the 2000s. Issues such as adverse selection,[41] unnecessary coverage (e.g., a woman who passes the age of menopause is still covered for pregnancy), and moral hazards[42] are just a few. Some argue that it is less expensive to pay for the individual violation penalty of $414, insurance copay, and deductible in case of medical needs than paying a monthly health insurance premium combined with out-of-pocket expenses, making the ACA not so affordable for many individuals. Others debate the constitutionality of forcing Americans to purchase insurance, let alone issues that revolve around insurance companies' pre-approval process (e.g., breast implants are covered by insurance only with proof of breast cancer).

---

[39]Ibid.

[40]Ibid.

[41]People with high health risk (e.g. diabetic) tend to purchase health insurance.

[42]People who have health insurance coverage tend to take less care of their health, especially for those who have low co-payment.

There is also growing concern about the quality of health care available to elderly people, particularly as the U.S. Government goes deeper into debt and tries to exercise measures to discount reimbursement under Medicare for heavily used, common medical procedures (e.g., hip and knee replacement).

Future Directions

Disparate opinions exist regarding the future of health care in America. To cut costs, some consider it important to provide patient care in patients' homes instead of hospitals. Kaiser Permanente is experimenting with ways to provide health care at home or on the Internet so patients do not need to go to a doctor's office. Telemedicine of this nature has its pros and cons, and is discussed further in Chapter 5. Halvorson (2013)[43] argues that finding ways to get people to take more responsibility for their health (e.g., lose weight and lower blood pressure) is key to lowering costs. With the computerization of healthcare records, privatizations/mergers of hospitals, legislative changes, and an aging population, the healthcare industry will continue to innovate toward valuing health where drug and pharmaceutical costs (for consumers/patients) should come down (even though it might increasingly become a more profitable segment of the overall healthcare industry) and access to quality care is easier for patients. Some argue that cost/care for each physician can be tracked and calculated easily due to computerization, providing insurance companies information for selecting doctors to be in-network. Mergers and acquisitions of different hospital chains, both in metropolitan areas and rural small towns, are already rapidly happening such that hospitals increase their bargaining power with insurance companies (or create their own in-house insurance plans to offer patients) on premiums. Others merge so that access to new segments of patients is possible. There will be continuous cost-cutting measures that restrict patient access to some specialists and medical hospitals due to negotiated prices regarding

---

[43]Reed Abelson, "The Face of Future Health Care," *The New York Times*, last updated March 20, 2013, accessed May 2, 2014, www.nytimes.com/2013/03/21/business/kaiser-permanente-is-seen-as-face-of-future-health-care.html?_r=0.

medical institutions/practices. The pros and cons of future development are multiple and vary depending on the entity's nature one serves. This chapter offers a brief overview of different typical hospital structures, how various divisions function to support each other, as well as the complex financing options. I also shared my perception of current controversy and future direction.

CHAPTER 2

How the Industry Operates

Traditionally, the healthcare industry is a hybrid of public and private services. Recently, it has grown more entrepreneurial, with increased emphasis on patient satisfaction and safety. This chapter aims at highlighting a few major elements that affect current operation of the industry: a brief review of historical changes, regulatory and compliance issues, different modes of operation and financing sources, impact of current health care financing on various constituents, as well as regulations pertaining to building codes and biomedical management.

History

Before 2010

U.S. spending on medical care has been on an upslope for a number of decades. In 1960, aggregate health expenditures in the United States were $27 billion. In 2003, the figure stood at nearly $1.7 trillion, a 63-fold rise. In contrast, the U.S. population grew by only 51 percent. Health expenditures per capita rose from $143 in 1960 to $5,670 in 2003, a 40-fold increase. General inflation pushed up prices of goods and services in the economy by 5-fold. In contrast, the recorded rise in prices for medical care was 12-fold, largely due to increases in hospital charges and doctors' fees.[1] The nation's healthcare spending tripled during the period, rising from approximately 5 percent of gross domestic product (GDP) in 1960 to over 15 percent in 2003.

Health care has and always will be one of the most debated political systems in America. Union negotiations during the 1940s reinforced the employment-based health insurance system. By the 1960s, the system of

[1]As measured by the Consumer Price Index for All-Urban Consumers, Bureau of Labor Statistics, U.S. Department of Labor.

private health insurance in United States was well established. However, there were many challenges. Those who worked for small companies or had no jobs had no health insurance. Those who retired and moved into old age also lost their health insurance. Medicare, provided by the government, particularly for those aged 65 and over, thus emerged.

During the 1970s, Presidents Nixon and Carter made various reforms to the national healthcare policy, and introduced the Medicare Part A payroll tax at 1.1 percent. Insurance coverage on prescription drug was introduced and cost sharing began. During the 1980s, the Consolidated Omnibus Budget Reconciliation Act of 1985 (COBRA) amended the Employee Retirement Income Security Act of 1974 (ERISA) to give some employees the option to continue health insurance coverage after leaving employment. During the 1990s, healthcare reform was a major agenda in the Clinton administration, but the 1993 Clinton healthcare plan was not enacted into law. The largest source of personal healthcare financing in the 2000s comes from private insurance, which furnished 36 percent of the funding for those expenditures in 2003. Out-of-pocket spending accounted for 16 percent, making it the next largest private source. Medicare and the federal share of Medicaid comprise the bulk of the federal government's support. The states' share of Medicaid is the largest component furnished by state and local governments. Table 2.1 summaries the national health expenditures over a 50 year period.

Table 2.1 National health expenditures from 1960–2014

Year	1960	1985	2003	2014
	(in billions of current dollars)			
Aggregate spending	27	427	1,679	3,031
Per capita	143	1,765	5,670	9,523
	(in billions of 2003 dollars)			
Aggregate spending	166	730	1,679	2,353
Per capita	891	3,019	5,670	7,392
	(in billions of 2014 dollars)			
Aggregate spending	214	945	2,163	3,031
Per capita	1,133	3,906	7,304	9,523
Share of GDP	5.1%	10.1%	15.3%	17.50%

www.cms.gov/Research-Statistics-Data-and-Systems/Statistics-Trends-and-Reports/NationalHealthExpendData/NationalHealthAccountsHistorical.html
www.cdc.gov/nchs/fastats/health-expenditures.htm

Table 2.2 Sources of financing of personal health care, 1960–2014

Year	1960	2003	2014
	Percent funded by		
Private insurance	21	36	33
Out of pocket	55	16	11
Medicare	–	19	20
Medicaid	–	17	16
Other private	2	4	13
Other federal	9	4	3
Other state and local	13	3	?
	(VA, DOD and CHIP section unaccounted)		

www.cms.gov/Research-Statistics-Data-and-Systems/Statistics-Trends-and-Reports/NationalHealthExpendData/Downloads/PieChartSourcesExpenditures2014.pdf

Table 2.2 above shows the change in the source of personal health care financing over five decades. The "Economic Survey of the United States 2008: Health Care Reform" by the Organization for Economic Cooperation and Development, states that:

- Tax benefits of employer-based insurances should be abolished.
- The resulting tax revenues should be used to subsidize the purchase of insurance by individuals.
- These subsidies, "which could take many forms, such as direct subsidies or refundable tax credits, would improve the current situation in at least two ways: they would reach those who do not now receive the benefit of the tax exclusion; and they would encourage more cost-conscious purchase of health insurance plans and healthcare services as, in contrast to the uncapped tax exclusion, such subsidies would reduce the incentive to purchase health plans with little cost sharing."[2]

[2]"Economic Survey of the United States 2008: Health Care Reform (December 9, 2008)," OECD, accessed May 22, 2014, www.keepeek.com/Digital-Asset-Management/oecd/economics/oecd-economic-surveys-united-states-2008_eco_surveys-usa-2008-en#page1.

After 2010

The Affordable Care Act (ACA) was passed into law in December 2009. Since then, multiple efforts have been made to both encourage and force every American to be covered by health insurance. To highlight a few, the pros of ACA regarding coverage, cost, and care include the following:

- Keeping young adults covered; those under 26 may be eligible for coverage under their parents' health insurance plans.
- Ending preexisting condition exclusions for children; health plans can no longer limit or deny benefits to children under 19 due to preexisting conditions.
- Ends lifetime limits on coverage; lifetime limits on most benefits are banned for all new health insurance plans.
- Removes limits on access to emergency services; one can seek emergency care at a hospital outside of one's health plan network.

For details on ACA and its update, refer to www.healthcare.gov/

Government Intervention

Policy

One of ACA's major requirements concerning patient protection is hospital compliance. Each healthcare institution is expected to adopt reasonable compliance standards of conduct and procedures, appoint a high-level compliance officer, provide employee education and systematic compliance training, develop audit and monitoring programs, develop mechanisms for reporting detected violation, and so on.[3] There will also be important changes regarding how the federal government pays for health care provided to Medicare beneficiaries. Apart from measures designed to lower fraud and waste in the current payment system. The

---

[3]Information about the guidelines for compliance can be found at the OIG website: http://oig.hhs.gov/fraud/complianceguidance.asp.

Act also provides demonstration projects that test reimbursement structures such as "bundled payments" and other risk-sharing setups among providers.

Other regulatory issues such as abuse, Stark, HIPAA privacy and security, EMTALA, and IRS requirements for tax-exempt organizations, and less common concerns that arise under antitrust laws, Red Flag Rules, and state insurance regulations, all need to be recognized. For example, criminal money laundering is the act of knowingly engaging in a monetary transaction in criminally derived property of a value greater than $10,000, and derived from specific unlawful activity (such as any act or activity constituting an offense involving a federal healthcare offense).[4] The Racketeer Influenced and Corrupt Organizations Act prohibits a person from receiving income from a pattern of activity, including committing an enumerated act (such as mail or wire fraud) at least twice in 10 years.[5] Under the False Claims Act (FCA), healthcare providers who knowingly make false or fraudulent claims to the government are fined $5,500 to $11,000 per claim, in addition to three times the amount of damages caused to the federal program.[6]

The Anti-Kickback Statue (AKS) and the Stark Physician Self-Referral Law (Stark Law) are two critical abuses and regulations. Stark prohibits physician referrals of designated health services (DHS) for Medicare and Medicaid patients if a physician (or an immediate family member) has a financial relationship with that entity. 42 U.S.C. 1395nn. A financial relationship includes ownership, investment interest, and compensation arrangements. 42 U.S.C. 1395nn(h)(5). AKS is intent based, so to violate the statue, a person must have the intent to give or receive remuneration for referrals.

Execution

The greatest risk for most healthcare organizations is fraudulent and inaccurate billing. Thus, the first step to compliance is to examine and analyze

---

[4] *Commodity Exchange Act, U.S. Code* 18 (1961), §§ 1956–1957.

[5] *Commodity Exchange Act,* §§ 1961 et seq.

[6] *Commodity Exchange Act, U.S. Code* 31, §§ 3729 et seq.

an organization's billing practices, under legal staff direction. On Medicare and Medicaid reimbursement issues, or other financial matters that have regulatory compliance implications, managers need to recognize and seek legal counsel before making decisions. On reimbursement arrangements, a single bundled payment means reimbursement for a continuum of inpatient hospital services, physician services, outpatient hospital services, and postacute care services for a scenario of care that begins three days before a hospitalization and spans 30 days after discharge. If bundled payment structures become a norm, relationships among institutional providers, physicians, outpatient clinics, and postacute care providers such as skilled nursing and home health care require a much higher level of integration and cooperation than existing networks in the current system.[7]

For FCA violations, intent to defraud the government is not required; the government needs only to establish evidence of a false claim, and that it was knowingly submitted. An amendment to the FCA was passed in 2009 that defines a claim under the FCA as a claim for payment made either directly to the government or to a government contractor. Thus, a bill ultimately (directly or indirectly) paid for by Medicare is available for prosecution under the FCA. Healthcare providers doing business with the government are expected to make at least basic audits regarding the accuracy of the claims they submit. Implementation of AKS and Stark law is challenging because requirements often contradict with economic interests of the parties structuring the relationships. There are also exceptions to the rule such as safe harbors, commentary to the rules, advisory opinions, and other published guidance. AKS is violated if one's purpose of the payment is to induce referrals.[8]

Impact

The United States spent nearly 17 percent of its GDP on health care (or over $7,000 on each American annually), nearly double the investment made in any other highly developed country,[9] but was ranked very

[7] *Patient Protection and Affordable Care Act,* Public Law 111–148, § 2704 (2010).
[8] *United States v. Kats,* 871 F.2d 105 (9th Cir. 1989).
[9] Centers for Medicare & Medicaid Services, Office of the Actuary, National Health Statistics Group (26), National Health Expenditure Projects 2009–2019, 4 (2010).

low on many standard measures of health status. The ACA is intended to put consumers in charge of their health care. Under the law, a new Patient's Bill of Rights gives Americans the flexibility to make informed decisions about their health. Some believe it is impossible to have coverage at a lower cost after implementation of ACA, and others believe it is unfair to have to pay a penalty for not having health insurance coverage. Nonetheless, taxpayers have the immediate impact of picking up the bill whether covered or uncovered Americans go to hospitals.[10] As an example, in Dallas, Texas, taxes from property owners is levied to finance uninsured people for health service, though the percentage is not significant. Time will reveal the true impact of the plan over the next decade.

Process Versus Value Focus

Process Measurement for Billing (Current)

One major issue in the U.S. healthcare system surfaces from the revenue generation cycle of related entities. Instead of paying healthcare entities for curing patients and their recovery, each procedure in the curing process is billable, offering unethical incentives for potentially unneeded tests and treatment. The current focus on process billing is problematic, expensive, and duplicative (at times), causing patients both financial and additional unnecessary physical strain. For example, treatment for a broken arm can involve the first step of an X-ray, confirming the fact/location of the fracture, costing $150 to $220. If it requires a CT scan for further diagnosis, an additional $500 to $1000 can be involved. So far, no treatment expense is discussed yet, but $200 to $1,200 is already incurred.[11] The current process does not encourage related entities that are treating a patient to communicate and exchange information for holistic treatment decisions. Instead, a patient can be asked to provide the same standard set of information/diagnostic records to three related but noncommunicating entities three times.

---

[10]John Iglehart, "Vision for Change in the U.S. Healthcare," *New England Journal of Medicine* (2009): 205–07.

[11]Henry C. Black, *The Law Dictionary*, 2nd ed. (Clark, NJ: The Lawbook Exchange, 1995), "How much money does it cost to fix a broken arm without health insurance?" p. 247.

Value Measurement for Result and Cost Reduction (Proposed)

According to Porter and Teisberg (2006), operations and patient treatment in healthcare units should be measured and compensated according to treatment results (e.g., non-readmittance level for the issue/sickness treated). A system that emphasizes results (patients' restored health) and cost reductions can then be put forth to begin eliminating waste in the industry overall. The focus needs to be on the full cycle of care instead of episodic, specific services. Generally, caring for a condition involves multiple doctor visits and many forms of treatment. The best way to maximize value for a patient is to have providers choose a combination of effort over the full cycle of care such that each treatment contributes to the overall treatment cycle, with the best results.

Full cycles of care are common in many countries. In the United States, it is currently up to the administration of healthcare entities to embrace the vision. Perhaps, the government's intervention in a supportive manner is needed at the policy level to help overcome political issues for such a concept to flourish in the country. An example piloted in the United States is the Integrated Healthcare Association (IHA) who served as the convener and lead organization for California's statewide Pay for Performance Program in 2001. Eight health plans and approximately 200 physician organizations participated in the program, which covered about 9 million Californians enrolled in commercial HMO and POS products. Seven of the plans have paid out over $450 million in incentives through 2012, based on results that have shown steady, incremental improvement in quality metrics.[12]

Privatization Versus Outsourcing

Whole Versus Partial Privatization

Privatization is the process of transferring productive operations and assets from the public to private sector. Currently, less than 20 percent,

[12]Jill Yeigan and Dolores Yanagihara, "Value-Based Pay for Performance: Rewarding Affordability Alongside Quality," *Health Affairs Blog,* last updated January 14, 2014, accessed March 20, 2014, http://healthaffairs.org/blog/2014/01/14/value-based-pay-for-performance-rewarding-affordability-alongside-quality/.

or not more than 800 hospitals, are owned by private, for-profit enterprises. However, there is an accelerating trend toward conversion of nonprofit or government-owned hospitals to private, for-profit hospitals in recent years. Generally, conversions are beneficial to both the general economy and the community involved regarding patient care and employee career opportunities. Hospital Corporation of America, a private hospital management company, took over the public Charity hospital in Louisiana. The result was improved overall healthcare quality and better working conditions for employees. In the case of a New Orleans hospital, about 90 percent of employees were hired back when it became privately owned. About 9 percent left the organization, and 1 percent lost their jobs due to system restructuring and elimination.

For many organizations, privatization requires phases. The University of Southern California (USC) University Hospital privatized several units of the USC hospital system over time.[13] There are pros and cons to partial/gradual privatization over the history of an organization. In the case of USC, its size and existing bureaucracy makes it challenging to complete full privatization as a single goal. Partial privatization can sometimes mean difficult management due to political interference by nonprivatized units. According to McDonald (1998), "to privatize hospital branches, individuals need to organize, weigh patient outcomes, adjust price bundles, integrate unified care, and grow excellent delivery."[14] Tradewell (1998) believes that it is simply more efficient for local government to obtain services from a regional, integrated care network than from a standalone public hospital. Privatization can raise cash, reduce debt, and create a better system for serving indigents. Moving from operating as a public hospital to a privatized system means crossing many regulations, meeting goals, negotiating the best deals, and handling union and public opposition.

---

[13]One can refer to Neith, "A New Era in USC Medicine," *University of Southern California* (June 2009), for a document of one phase of privatization.

[14]Kevin McDonald, "Why Privatization Is Not Enough," *Harvard Business Review* (May–June 1993): 38–41.

Effectiveness Versus Efficiency Focus

Efficiency involves ways to improve speed and completing business tasks, and effectiveness focuses on evaluating existing procedures and uncovering new ways to service business needs better. During hospital privatization, effectiveness can be translated as increased operating margins, reduced length of stay, and higher occupancy rates. Efficiency often refers to reduced debt, raised capital, and a better system for serving indigent people. In the past, the rationale for healthcare providers to undertake quality improvement initiatives rested largely on "doing the right thing"; resulting financial benefits were an attractive side effect. A new approach to the business is systematic identification and elimination of waste while maintaining and improving quality. Thus, management and statistical foci on quality improvement such as Six Sigma are gaining popularity in the healthcare industry.

Healthcare Financing

Health care is rapidly changing in terms of how and where care is delivered, who provides services, and how care is financed. These changes are driven primarily by growth of managed care. There are two general approaches to financing health care: market-based and government-financed. They each offer various advantages and disadvantages, and neither approach is perfect. Every society, community, or country must decide on the scope of basic versus advanced care provided to its citizens, and the types and expenses budgeted for innovation made available to patients.

In a market-based system, care is generally delivered by private organizations and individuals, and all parts of the system are subject to some degree of competition. The variety of providers, suppliers, and payers can be huge. Insured patients are free to choose their service providers without limits. Doctors are free to make treatment/care decisions on a case-by-case basis, considering the unique needs of individual patients. Financial incentives exist to develop new medical advances to bring the best new products to customers. Instead of being cost focused, customers make choices based on many variables such as quality, service, and convenience.

In a government-financed system, some basic level of care is provided to all. The system is financed through taxes and other charges. The government might deliver the care itself, as in the United Kingdom, or it might contract with other providers to offer the service, as in German and Japanese systems. In the United States, Medicare and Medicaid serve such functions. Given the scope and reach of a government-financed system, more limitations are usually placed on the range of care offered and the choices of doctors available to keep costs down. Generally, it takes longer for new advances to be accepted and reimbursed by the government, and therefore longer to become available to physicians and patients. Consequently, diagnostics and treatments that are offered might not be the same as what is available in a market-based system.[15]

What is Measured/Billed?

The Office of the Actuary at the Health Care Financing Administration (HCFA) documents most expenditures on health care in the United States. Personal healthcare data in National Health Expenditure estimates are commonly reported in nine categories: hospital care, physician services, dental services, other professional services, home healthcare, nursing home care, drugs and other medical nondurables, vision products, and other medical durables. However, the expense of private insurance and private out of pocket is usually unavailable from government surveys and trade associations, suggesting underreporting of the amount spent on health care. When it comes to billing, a general hospital bill consists of payments to physicians for services performed, consumables related to diagnosis, equipment and treatment, and overhead charges such as lodging and food. From time to time, instances of exaggerated pricing on disposables such as gloves ($53/pair) and syringes ($11 each), or huge price differences for the same procedure, are reported in the news,[16] though it is not the norm. The issue lies in policies and systems applied to categories of patients with disparate coverage/

[15]Michael Nowicki, *The Financial Management of Hospitals and Healthcare Organizations* (Chicago: Health Administration Press, 2004), 267.

[16]Sarah Cliff and Dan Keating, "One Hospital Charges $8,000—Another, $38,000," *Washington Post,* last updated May 8, 2013, accessed April 29, 2014, www.washingtonpost.com/blogs/wonkblog/wp/2013/05/08/one-hospital-8000-another-38000/.

rates of reimbursement to hospitals. It is important that patients learn about the treatment/expenses involved, and negotiate at times, to ensure they are not burdened with a lifelong debt after treatment.

Impact on Hospital

Typical hospitals have the financial goal to 1) maintain operating viability, 2) maintain favorable bond and borrowing ratings, and 3) define full charges as a benchmark for negotiating discounts and fees with insurers. Capital is needed to fund physician employment and integration, information technology, facility modernization and expansion, and other initiatives. Forward-looking hospitals make substantial capital investments in all of these areas. The trend of physician employment has evolved to be contract based in many hospitals. Kaiser Permenante is an exception. Since mid-2008, constrained national liquidity has made it more difficult for capital access; fewer borrowing options, more restrictive terms, higher risks related to available borrowing options, higher cost of capital, and less flexibility make it more challenging for hospitals to access capital, particularly for smaller hospitals.[17] To ensure capital options in the new healthcare environment, leadership teams need to recognize the need to access external capital. It follows that in-depth understanding of current and future financial and strategic positions, credit position preservation, and close monitoring of existing funds and new opportunities are essential.

Impact on Physician

Following enactment of ACA, physicians, especially those in private practice, have hundreds of pages more of regulations for interpretation, so there is urgent need to simplify the complexity of ACA. Although the total number of uninsured people has gone down, there are regulations underway to replace the ACA package, potentially making health care

[17]Kaufman, Hall & Associates, Inc., *A Guide to Financing Strategies for Hospitals With Special Consideration for Smaller Hospitals* (Chicago: Kaufman, Hall & Associates, Inc., 2010), 179.

more unaffordable for some.[18] Expanding access, particularly in rural areas, remains a top priority for policymakers. Some physicians would rather refrain from administration of insurance, and charge patients who need help using a flat rate treatment plan or cash rate basis. Although there was a former trend for physicians to specialize in subspecialty areas of medicine after completing general medical training for both personal aspirations and remuneration potential (and this trend will likely continue),[19] recent changes (e.g., billing complexity, lack of control of reimbursement rate from the government and insurance companies, etc.) is prompting more medical students to reconsider general family physician as a career due to better opportunities for revenue generation. It is challenging to keep abreast of the daily changes that are taking place in the medical industry. It will continue to be challenging for any medical practitioner to strike a balance between advancing their professional expertise and being informed of regulatory changes.

Impact on Patient

Patient care is a direct source of income for hospitals, generally. Hospitals' foci on any facility upgrade and patient satisfaction center on attracting more patients to use hospital services for increased income and leveraging economies of scale. Under the Affordable Care Act (ACA), a person earning about $46,000 for a single household or $94,000 for a family of four were eligible for government subsidy to help them buy insurance coverage in 2014. If one were eligible for the subsidy, one had the option of having the subsidy on one's federal tax return or applied directly to monthly health insurance premiums. If one qualifies for additional subsidy to help lower copayments and deductibles, those funds will be provided directly from the government to the health insurance company.[20]

---

[18]Timothy Jost, "An Affordable Care Act at Year 5: Key Issues for Improvement," *JAMA* 313, no. 17 (May 5, 2015): 1709–10.

[19]Collin P. West and Denise M. Dupras, "General Medicine vs Subspecialty Career Plans Among Internal Medicine Residents," *JAMA* 308, no. 21 (December 5, 2012): 2241–47.

[20]"2014 Health Insurance Subsidies FAQ," eHealth, last modified December 23, 2013, accessed May 28, 2014, www.ehealthinsurance.com/afforabable-care-act/news/2014-health-insurance-subsidies-faq.

The American Academy of Physician Assistants supports many provisions of the Patient Protection and Affordable Care Act (PPACA), which makes significant effort to expand the roles of primary care medicine and team-based health care, expand preventive screenings and treatments to all patients, and increase access to quality health care in underserved communities. It also encourages growth of health information technology, and addresses health disparities. See an article by Cutler (2015) titled "From the Affordable Care Act to Affordable Care" for more information about patient protection, malpractice, spending, and the Affordable Care Act.

Impact on Taxpayer

The issue of how much financial resources should be spent on health care is an important societal challenge. Under the ACA, there is a massive increase in Medicare and government subsidies, which come directly from taxpayers.[21] According to data available from the Joint Committee on Taxation (2010), 17 new taxes/penalties will be added, and the annual tax spending as a result of Obamacare will rise from approximately \$19 million in 2011 to about \$110 million in 2019 (more than a 450% increase over eight years).

The PPACA promises enhancement of providers' integrity obligations and extension of the federal government's anti-fraud and abuse capabilities. Tax-exempt hospitals are required to conduct assessments of community needs and address them. Each hospital is required to submit an annual report describing the identity of ownership and the nature and extent of all physician ownership in a hospital.[22]

Impact on Other Related and Supporting Industries

Significant improvements to healthcare workforce development are expected in the next 5–10 years. Creation of the American Health Benefit

---

[21]Alyene Senger, "Obamacare's Impact on Today's and Tomorrow's Taxpayers," last modified August 21, 2013, accessed May 25, 2014, www.heritage.org/research/re-ports/2013/08/obamacares-impact-on-todays-and-tomorrows-taxpayers-an-update.

[22]Hall XII, "Survey of Recent Developments in Health Care Law," *Health Law,* 2011-01-1.

Exchanges and Small Business Health Options Program Exchanges means there is also a provision for every state to have a public health insurance exchange to facilitate individual and small employers' purchases of qualified health plans. Most of the exchanges will be run by the Health and Human Services (HHS) or a partnership between the state and HHS, except 17 states that run their own exchanges. These exchanges will be marketplaces for both individual and small-group health insurance. Although they are called public exchanges, the health plans are offered by private health insurance carriers, including many brand-name carriers known commonly in the industry.[23] Under this system, people will be able to shop within their state's exchanges and choose from a variety of qualified health plans. The exchanges will be places at which applicants compare and enroll in plans, and receive premiums and cost-sharing subsidies on eligibility verification.[24]

Suppliers of medical products, technology, and services are constituents that will greatly benefit from the new policies. They play vital roles in the delivery and innovation of value health care. As a key stakeholder, this group can add far more value to healthcare delivery than they have yet realized.

Physical Plant and New Building Codes

It is important for healthcare administrators to understand physical plants and building codes required for designing disaster-resistant facilities. The UCLA Ronald Reagan hospital (earthquake-proof requirement after 1995) and the Medical University of South Carolina's (MUSC) new Courtenay building (hurricane-proof requirement after 2005), both opened after 2008, are two examples for national benchmarking. After the

---

[23]As of July 2015, a report is released about health exchange's inability to detect fake claims, resulting in $30,000 in subsidies that are paid to insurers. The Centers for Medicare and Medicaid Services (CMS) acknowledged limited ability to respond to fraud attempt (Stephanie Armour, "Health Exchange Approved Fake Claims," *The Wall Street Journal* A3, last updated July 16, 2015).

[24]Lawrence O. Gostin et al., "Restoring Health to Health Reform: Integrating Medicine and Public Health to Advance the Population's Well-Being," *University of Pennsylvania Law Review* 159, no. 6 (2011): 1777–1823.

1994 Northridge earthquake, hospitals in California (CA) are required to withstand natural disasters, specifically to endure immense earthquakes. They must meet CA's seismic safety standards of resisting 8.0 Richter magnitude earthquake, and remain fully operational, independent of outside resources, for the crucial 72 hours following a major earthquake. Basic performance standards require the new building to withstand winds of 70 mph and driving rain conditions.[25]

Assembled above underground faults and on unstable soil, MUSC is unreliable in the event of a hurricane due to possible flooding. Thus, the city's updated building codes require hospitals to be hurricane and flood resistant, similar to requirements for costal CA standards. The new building can withstand winds in excess of 130 mph and major earthquake conditions. During a natural disaster, wings of the building can shake and be slightly shifted apart by inches, but still not break, and remain operational. The roof of the building was also designed for helicopter landings for disaster relief. In the case of MUSC, since it is located in Charleston, strict limits are set on the height of the hospital to comply with local architectural regulations. Healthcare administrators need to be versed in their local city limits and regulations. The leadership team also needs to be prepared for many political meetings and negotiations before financing and other resources are secured for construction of physical projects of this nature.

Hazardous and Biowaste Treatment

Biomedical waste is potentially infectious material that is restricted from environmental release, whether from research laboratories, medical institutions, or other origins. Some hospitals use a combination of external vendors for off-site treatment and on-site sterilization, and mobile sterilization units. In the risk management section of hospital policy, management can state the spill plan, a contingency plan for alternative treatment, storage and disposal sites, handling and storage of infectious waste, radiological monitoring, and personnel health and safety training.

[25]UCLA Health, "Ronald Reagan UCLA Medical Center," accessed March 10, 2014, www.uclahealth.org/body_med.cfm?=903.

In 1988, the United States passed the Medical Waste Tracking Act, which set standards for governmental regulation of medical waste. After the Act expired in 1991, states were given the responsibility to regulate and pass laws concerning disposal of medical waste.[26]

This chapter offers a brief overview of the development of the field over time, and discusses legislative influences and issues regarding financing and operation of hospitals.

[26]Environmental Protection Agency, "Guidelines for the Management of Biomedical Waste in the Northwest Territories," accessed May 28, 2014, www.enr.gov.nt.ca/sites/dafult/files/guidelines/biomedical_waste.pdf.

CHAPTER 3

Industry Organization and Competition

Industry Structure

In chapter 1, we explore several hospital structures—privately owned, government owned, and university-based teaching hospitals that include both a public and private wing. This chapter discusses a health delivery system that involves more than the hospital itself, but interrelated players. According to Porter and Lee (2013), health care organized among vertically integrated groups (VIG) is a strategy that will fix health care.[1]

Vertically Integrated Groups

VIGs are institutions that perform a series of functions within the healthcare delivery system. Sentara is one that integrates with the healthcare insurance market, medical schools, and other areas among them. In 1990s, before electronic health records (EHR) was mandatory, it had already starting thinking about EHR.[2] Intermountain Health Care is another vertically integrated group that owns 23 hospitals and an insurance company called SelectHealth with approximately 500,000 members.[3]

---

[1]Michael E. Porter and Thomas H. Lee, "The Strategy That Will Fix Healthcare," *Harvard Business Review* (October 2013): 1–9.

[2]John Morrissey, "Before They Were Famous: Sentara's Bernd Started Thinking About EHRs As Far Back As 1992," *Modern Healthcare* 40, no. 24 (June 14, 2010): 1.

[3]Leigh Page, "50 Integrated Delivery Systems to Know," *Beckers Hospital Review*, last modified October 14, 2010, accessed March 12, 2014, www.beckershospitalreview.com/hospital-physician-relationships/50-integrated-delivery-system-to-know.html.

Integrated Practice Units

Integrated Practice Units (IPUs) such as Cleveland Clinic use a group practice model that combines specialists of organs into patient care groups to provide collaborative care for patients. Doctors are paid a flat rate regardless of the number of patients treated. IPUs integrate several elements in the care delivery system, with a focus on quality. Areas integrated include the following:

- Information technology
- Cost and outcomes measurement
- Bundled payments
- Integrated care deliveries across facilities
- Expanded service across geography

New England Baptist Hospital is another IPU that competes to be the best in one area (e.g., orthopedics, musculoskeletal care, and others) in the medical industry by merging with Beth Israel Deaconess Medical Center.[4]

Information Providers

ThedaCare is a major player in the industry whose information-provider network role provides public information for patients to make the best informed decision, leading to higher quality care and patient satisfaction. Every year, there are about fifteen million instances of medical harm in this country, including drug errors, infections, and wrong-side surgeries. Throughout care delivery, doctors, nurses, and technicians are hamstrung by outmoded, cobbled-together systems that encourage waste and restrict the most important constituents in medicine—the patient. It is worth benchmarking this Wisconsin example (ThedaCare) because it liaises with other information providers to offer the community information on provider performance. This arrangement creates competition among companies,

[4]Melissa Malamot, "Beth Israel Deaconess and New England Baptist Partnership," *Boston Magazine,* last modified February 11, 2014, accessed March 09, 2016, www.bostonmagazine.com/health/blog/2014/02/11/beth-israel-deaconess-new-england-baptist-orthopedic-partnership/.

possibly driving prices down and resulting in more choices and better quality care for patients.[5]

Brands and Branding Strategies—A Highly Fragmented Industry

Although most hospitals and medical facilities serve similar functions such as patient care, research, and training, institutions located in disparate regions usually have their own priorities and specialties based on historical roots, organizational strategy, resources, and expertise availability. The top three competitors in the United States that offer nationwide medical services are Johns Hopkins, Cleveland Clinic, and the Mayo Clinic.[6] They all share similar organizational structures and are trying to expand nationwide. Johns Hopkins specializes in research because it has a medical school, and thus education and training of new generations of medical professionals is its priority. The Mayo Clinic establishes its brand name for patient focus and satisfaction. Cleveland Clinic specializes in the cardiac field, and is a national leader in prevention, evaluation, and treatment of cardiovascular disease.

The four typical types of ownership in most hospitals are privately owned, nonprofit, for-profit, and government-owned. For example, the Mayo Clinic and Cleveland Clinic are both nonprofit and privately owned medical practices. Johns Hopkins is also nonprofit, but is run and owned by a university. An example of a government-owned hospital is Broward Health based in South Florida, which is one of the largest medical facilities in the country. Generally, government hospitals are the most abundant and affordable for the public.[7]

The healthcare industry is highly fragmented, with no dominant players, partially due to the geographic/proximity needs and nature of urgency in health care. It is characterized by organization type, range of services

---

[5]John Toussaint, "Writing the New Playbook for U.S. Health Care: Lessons from Wisconsin Health Affairs," *Health Affairs* 28, no. 5 (2009): 1343–50.

[6]Andrew Owens, "Mayo Merger," *PostBulletin.com,* last modified July 28, 2011, accessed April 28, 2014, www.postbulletin.com/news/local/mayo-merger-mayo-clinic-s-governing-structure-has-evolved-since/article_736f464f-0fee-5741-9fc0-31e197ba1990.html.

[7]"Public Health," *SafetyNetsFlorida.org,* accessed April 28, 2014, safetynetsflorida.org/public.

offered, and variation in prices. What follows is a rough attempt to show three hospital types and their respective target segments and average prices.

Table 3.1. Hospital type/segment served

Type	*Example of Range of Services*	*Corresponding Price*	*Main Function*	*Class*
A private medical center	Full range service focused on one specialty organ 1. The examination 2. The surgery 3. Pre and Posttreatment care 4. Sale of equipment to support the normal function of the organ post-surgery	1. \$25 2. \$3995 flat cash rate combined with surgery 3. \$1000 4. Prices vary based on type, style and brand Prices fixed regardless of insurance plans	Provide high-quality patient care services and consultation, with extensive focus on research and education.	Upper
A community hospital	1. Cardiovascular services 2. Diabetes education 3. Digital Cardiac Testing 4. Stroke services 5. Occupational Therapy 6. Hospitalist service 7. Birthing Center 8. Neurology 9. Dieticians services 10. Home medical equipment 11. Prompt care 12. Aquatic Therapy 13. Joint replacement 14. Sports health clinic 15. Pastoral care 16. Surgical weight loss 17. Exercise classes[8]	1. \$4K 2. \$5K 3. \$300 4. \$700 5. \$6K 6. \$50 7. \$4K 8. \$120K 9. \$400 10. Price varies by equipment 11. \$50 12. \$400 13. \$5K 14. \$1K 15. \$100 16. \$5K 17. \$40 Prices vary depending on insurance plans	Provide comprehensive healthcare services to the local community. As part of a larger healthcare system, staff in this medical center strives to serve every patient, every time with the greatest care and love.	Middle/ Lower

[8]SF St. Joseph Medical Center, *osfstjoseph.org*, accessed March 6, 2014.

A state/ university–funded medical hospital and center	1. Knee replacement 2. Stroke treatment 3. Birthing As this is a teaching hospital, the list of services available goes above 85, ranging from A (AIDS) to W (wound care); thus, one can refer to any teaching hospital service for the details.	1. \$20–35K+; with insurance: 4,500 (out-of-pocket) 2. \$150–3000 (for emergency room), *5K or more for hospitalization. 3. \$9k–25K; with insurance: 200–500 (bill for new born not included yet).	Provide its students with medical education and research the latest treatment for advanced illness.	Varies

Table 3.1 is a rough attempt in showing some of the range of different services offered by various hospital types and segments. The private medical center offers only limited services, but is recognized as a high-quality brand, with specialization in one organ while a full range of services is available at its specialty. The community hospital offers many services, all of which cannot fit in a table. It is nonprofit and offers many cost-efficient healthcare options for people in two neighboring communities. The university hospital offers the widest range of services for a community that spans a 250-mile radius (e.g., Neonatal center level 4). Both the breadth and depth of services offered makes it a much-needed hospital for the community and neighboring cities, regardless of financial status.

Service Tiers

Apart from general hospitals, specialty hospitals provide personalized care for patients that would not necessarily be offered at general hospitals, including daily physician visits, multi-specialty medical and surgical consultants, low patient-to-nurse ratios, 24-hour nursing and respiratory services, on-site physical, speech, and occupational therapies, on-site pharmacies, cardiac monitoring, specialized medical equipment, diagnostic services, laboratory services, interdisciplinary team management, registered dieticians, case management, and discharge planning.[9] Most specialty hospitals serve patients who require a

[9] "Services," *SelectSpecialtyHospitals.com,* last modified April 20, 2014, accessed April 29, 2014, www.selectspecialtyhospitals.com/services/.

high degree of care that cannot be provided from general, short-term-care hospitals. Examples include ventilated patients, trauma victims, extensive wound care, and transplant patients.[10] They are distributed around the country, with 28 states having at least one specialty hospital. However, approximately two-thirds of specialty hospitals are located in seven states—Arizona, California, Kansas, Louisiana, Oklahoma, South Dakota, and Texas—due to state regulations/restrictions regarding hospital growth.

Specialty hospitals are much less likely to have emergency departments, treat smaller percentages of Medicaid patients, and derive a smaller share of revenue from inpatient services. For example, 45 percent of specialty hospitals, but 92 percent of general hospitals, have emergency departments. Although general hospitals typically have more beds than specialty hospitals, the focused mission of specialty hospitals often results in treating more patients in their given fields of specialization. Financially, specialty hospitals perform about as well as general hospitals do on their Medicare, inpatient business. However, specialty hospitals outperform general hospitals when costs from all lines of business and revenues from all payers are considered.[11] Specialty hospitals accounted for about 1 percent of Medicare's spending on hospital inpatient services in 2001. Over 70 percent have some form of ownership by physicians. Policies regarding preventing conflicts of interest should be in place in specialty hospitals so there will not be referral of unnecessary cases to specialty hospitals for treatment/revenue-generation reasons. Chart 3.2 summarizes the pros and cons of specialty hospitals.[12]

---

[10]"The Specialty Hospital of Washington," *Specialhospitalofwashington.com,* accessed April 10, 2014, www.specialtyhospitalofwashington.com/types-of-patients-we-serve/.

[11]"Geographic Location, Services Provided, and Financial Performance," The General Accounting Office, last modified October 2003, accessed April 22, 2014, http://gao.gov/new.items/d04167.pdf.

[12]Ann Tynan,"General Hospitals, Specialty Hospitals and Financially Vulnerable Patients," *HSChange.com,* last modified April 10, 2014, accessed April 30, 2014, www.hschange.com/CONTENT/1056/.

Policy Context
The Pros and cons of Specialty Hospitals

PROS	CONS
• Drawing on the theory of focused factories, proponents contend that specialty hospitals can secure high volumes, thereby improving quality and reducing costs. • Specialty hospitals may raise the bar for quality and encourage general hospitals to implement quality improvement strategies to compete effectively. • Specialty hospitals offer patients better amenities and achieve higher patient satisfaction. • Specialty hospitals offer physicians greater control over management decisions affecting productivity and quality.	• Specialty hospitals tend to treat lower-acuity, well-insured patients while avoiding uninsured and Medicaid patients. • Opponents contend that specialty hospital competition threatens the ability of general hospitals to cross-subsidize less-profitable services and patients. • Specialty hospitals may be unable to manage emergencies effectively as some do not have physicians on site at all times. • Ownership structure of specialty hospitals may encourge physician self-referrals and overutilization of services.

Sources: Department of Health and Human Services: Office of the Inspector General, OEI-02-06-00310, *Physician-Owned Specialty Hospitals' Ability to Manage Medical Emergencies* (January 2008); Choudry, Sujit, Niteesh K. Choudry, and Troyen A. Brennan, "Specialty Versus Community Hospitals: What Role for the Law?" *Health Affairs*, Web exclusive (Aug. 9, 2005); Gram, Peter, et al., "Insurance Status of Patients Admitted To Specialty Cardiac And Competing General Hospitals: Are Accusations Of Cherry Picking Justified." *Medical Care*, Vol. 46, No. 5 (May 2008); Devers, Kelly, Linda R. Brewster and Paul B. Ginsburg, *Specialty Hospitals: Focused Factories or Cream Skimmers?* Issue Brief No. 62, Center for Studying Health System Change, Washington, D.C. (April 2003); Greenwald, Leslie, et al., "Specialty Versus Community Hospitals: Referrals, Quality, and Community Benefits," *Health Affairs*, Vol. 25, No. 1 (January/February 2006).

Figure 3.2. Pros and cons of specialty hospital

Uniqueness of the Healthcare Service

The healthcare industry is uniquely part service (i.e., medical professionals' expert knowledge during diagnosis, treatment plans, medication prescriptions, and continuous consultations concerning progress/recovery) and part goods (i.e., drugs and medical equipment), in which one cannot function in full without the other. The goods and services are not only complementary, but they are nearly indispensable for one another. It is also an industry in which time is critical since delay during an emergency can result in drastic differences in outcome, and possibly death. With newly developed diseases/viruses, and new treatment possibilities from research, it is also critical that continuous education on both new drugs and treatments be maintained.

From a management perspective, health care resides in the service industry, in which a product sold is intangible and the offering is an experience of a series of various elements over time. Unlike a plane ride, during which a passenger's experience lasts for hours or days at most, healthcare services can be an experience that ranges from hours to years, depending on the type of illness involved, and the healing process undertaken. Continuous consumption of both medication and services (e.g., diagnostic updates, consultations, and therapies) at numerous facilities and with various professionals at varying degrees of expertise and competency over time complicates evaluation of the overall patient experience.

From a patient perspective, if a patient suffers a relapse after changing geographical locations, there will be many additional steps involved. For example, the request for release of former medical records, and identification of a new team of medical professionals for treatment (who are willing to communicate with former physicians on the patient's request). All these can become another project that redefines the patient's experience. One study suggests that hospital employees' energy and personalities shape a patient's experience.[13] Another study suggests that health information technology (HIT) reliability, which reduces bottlenecks and scheduling conflicts, is pivotal to building a patient's confidence and loyalty with a hospital.[14]

Generally, one easily assumes that a patient's experience depends largely on the medical professionals' expertise and the staff team's competency. However, "patient as part of the delivery process" is a concept that many miss; a patient can buy the best medical staff and treatment in the world, but one can still have a poor patient experience and health outcome if one does not follow the physicians' prescription on medication and dietary/exercise routines.

Another stakeholder in the healthcare experience of a patient is his/her community/family. If one has supportive community/family, one's healing process (regardless of the recovery rate) and patient experience can be much more positive. One's emotional and spiritual health, particularly during physical health recovery, can be volatile and be influenced by (un)supportive community relationships in either direction to help/worsen

---

[13]Brian R. Needham, "The Truth About Patient Experience: What We Can Learn from Other Industries, and How Three Ps Can Improve Health Outcomes, Strengthen Brands, and Delight Customers," *Journal of Healthcare Management* 57, no. 4 (2012): 255–63.

[14]Brian Kolowitz et al., "Workflow Continuity-Moving Beyond Business Continuity in a Multisite 24-7 Healthcare Organization," *Journal of Digital Imaging* 25, no. 6 (2012): 744–50.

healing. This explains why many hospitals have increasingly invested in spiritual services and patient family support over the last few decades.

Human Resource Management

Health care is a labor-intensive industry. Both high- and low-skill staff members are required to facilitate patient safety and satisfaction. Broadly, healthcare workers are divided into two categories: practitioners/technical and support. In 2014, approximately 9 percent (healthcare practitioner and technical, 5.8%; healthcare support, 2.9%) of total U.S. employment was in health care, after sales and related industries, and office administration.[15] Of the top 10 most expected job growth areas for 2012 to 2022, five are healthcare related (i.e., registered nurse, home health aid, secretaries in medical industry, personal care aids, and nurse assistants).[16] Management of human resources in the healthcare industry is a challenging task because of evolving dynamics regarding recruitment, training, and retention, and changing legislation that regulates the industry, in addition to typical labor relations.

In terms of labor availability, although we continue to train locally and recruit internationally, Chart 3.3 shows that there is still high demand for labor in the healthcare industry.[17] Nurse practitioners, physician assistants; physical therapists, assistants, and aides; home health aids, and personal care aids will experience the greatest shortages, projected through 2024. Chart 3.4 shows average earnings and respective employment size of healthcare professionals and support workers.[18] A registered nurse shortage has been ongoing. Recently, worsening work conditions and changing standards in the nursing profession from personal care

---

[15]United States Department of Labor, "Occupational Employment and Wages in Cape Coral-Fort Myers—May 2014," accessed June 30, 2015, www.bls.gov/regions/south-east/newsrelease/occupationalemploymentandwages_capecoral.htm.

[16]United States Department of Labor, "Fastest Growing Occupations, 2014–24," last modified December 19, 2013, accessed July 1, 2015, www.bls.gov/news.release/ecopro.t05.htm.

[17]United States Department of Labor, "Health Care," *Spotlight on Statistics,* last modified February, 2015, accessed June 20, 2016, www.bls.gov/spotlight/2015/health_care/.

[18]Ibid.

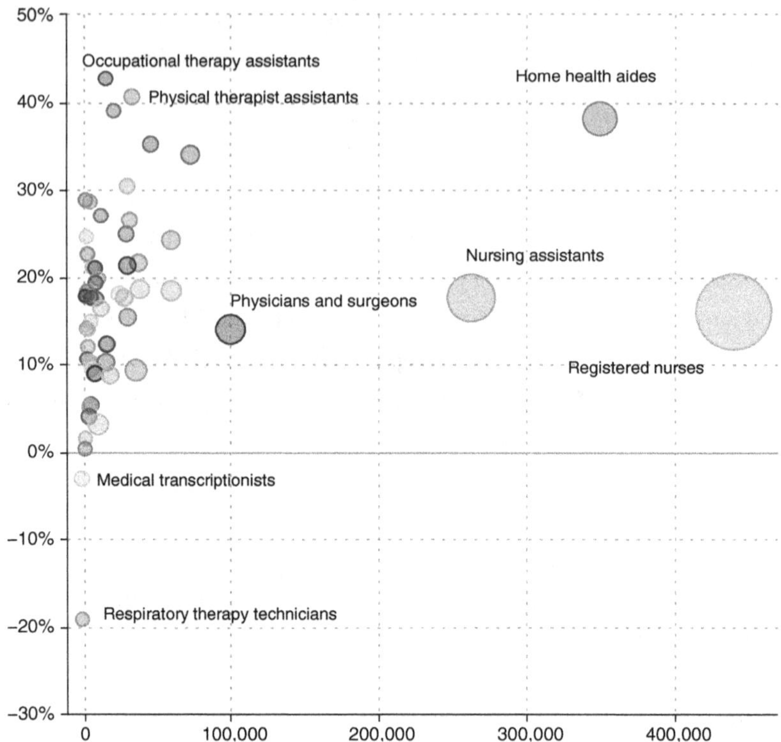

Chart 3.3 Projected change in total employment, selected health care occupations
Source: Employment Projections | Chart Data.

to impersonal administration exacerbate it. There is a mix of increased younger generations entering the nursing profession for an attractive remuneration package, but there remains a shortage of nurses because many employers are unwilling to hire new graduates without experience. For home health and personal care aids, the shortage derives from soaring demand from the United States' fast-aging population. Although there is a constant supply of workforces entering the market, the supply is still growing slower than demand.

Shortage of Nursing Staff

The shortage of nursing staff across the board is a major concern for hospitals because it influences patient safety and quality of care. Some adverse patient outcomes related to nursing-sensitive indicators include

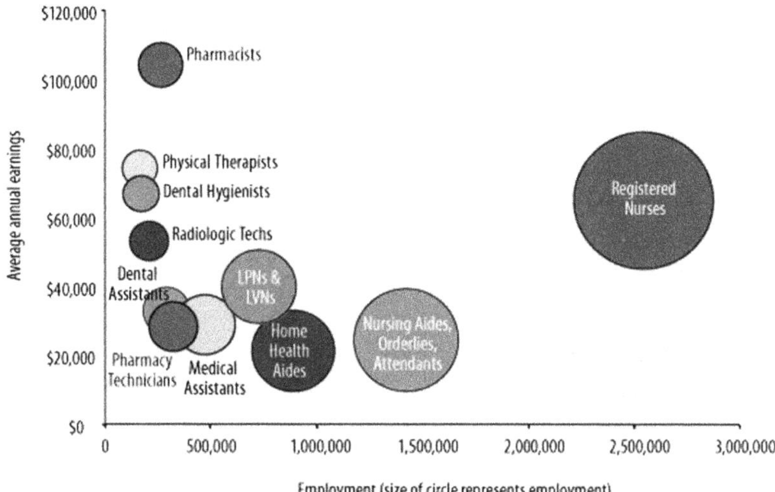

Chart 3.4 Employment and earnings

Source: Occupational Employment Statistics | Chart Data

urinary tract infections (UTIs), pneumonia, shock, upper gastrointestinal bleeding, longer hospital stays, failure to rescue, and 30-day mortality. The current nursing shortage is a result of fundamental changes to population demographics, career expectations, work attitudes, and worker dissatisfaction. Although some hospitals provide continuous educational opportunities for nurses, others do not.[19] A federal government study predicts that hospital nursing vacancies will reach 29 percent by 2020. The number of nurses is expected to grow by only 6 percent by 2020, while demand for nursing care is expected to grow by 40 percent.[20] The annual nursing staff turnover rate averages about 18 percent.[21]

Physician Training

The degree of care and competency expected from practitioners is reflected in training to serve the public. Chart 3.5 shows one of the many training

[19]M. L. Garahani, "Educational Practices Accomplished by Hospital Nurses Published in National Journals," *Ciencia* (2009): 1.

[20]Mark Stanton, "Hospital Nurse Staffing and Quality of Care," *Research in Action,* no. 14 (March, 2004).

[21]Madeleine Estryn-Behar, "Longitudinal Analysis of Personal and Work-Related Factors Associated with Turnover Among Nurses," *Nursing Research* (2010).

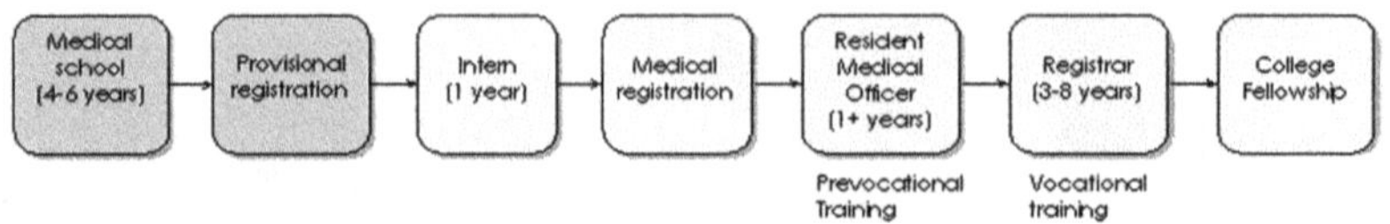

Chart 3.5 Training and education of physician

paths of an aspiring doctor. After completion of a Bachelor's degree, a doctor still has up to 14 more years of education/training prior to practicing in the profession independently. Physicians who go into specialized fields may receive even more years of fellowship/training. The investment needed to become a physician indirectly suggests the importance of this industry to the United States. After licensing as a professional in a field, a doctor also needs to continue with education and remain updated to maintain the license.

Most hospitals report a 13 percent discrepancy in staff, meaning hospitals are understaffed regarding physicians and nurses.[22] From 2009 to 2014, U.S. medical school graduates grew from approximately 71,000 to 78,000, specialties programs increased from 4,128 to 4,286, and subspecialties programs grew from 4,745 to 5,482.[23]

Technological Change in the Healthcare Industry

The Health Insurance Portability and Accountability Act of 1996 (HIPPA) was enacted to improve the effectiveness and efficiency of the healthcare system by encouraging development of a health information system through standards and requirements for electronic transmission of health information.[8] The American Recovery and Reinvestment Act of 2009 contains the Health Information Technology for Economic and Clinical Health Act (HITECH Act), which authorizes significant investment in health information technology and expands the provisions of

[22]"Evergreen Healthcare Partners with API Healthcare to Get Labor Productivity and Costs Under Control," *Health & Beauty Close-Up* (March 2, 2012), http://search.proquest.com.proxy.pba.edu/docview/925655472?accountid=26397.

[23]Colin P. West and Denise M. Dupras, "General Medicine vs Subspecialty Career Plans Among Internal Medicine Residents," *JAMA* 308, no. 21 (2012): 2241–47.

[24]Public Law 104–191, 110 Stat. 1936 (1996).

HIPPA.[9] As its name suggests, Health Information Exchange refers to the exchange of health information among electronic health record systems. HIE is an ideal scenario that will take some time to realize since many electronic health record systems are not designed for information exchange/integration. Over the last few decades, HIE continues to be an initiative that many hospitals strive to perfect. However, adoption by organizations and departments varies greatly due to challenges commonly experienced regarding lack of supportive organization cultures for full implementation (Sultz and Young, 2014). In an integrated HIE model, a patient who has medical records in a number of institutions (e.g., community hospital, department of health, reference laboratory, university medical center, private physician group, etc.) will have his/her records updated and channeled into a central database (i.e., one large HIE database) regularly so authorized users can access it as needed. Recently, Unique Device Identification (UDI) of medical components and parts has been suggested by the Food and Drug Administration (FDA) to be incorporated in the HIE system to reduce medical errors, reduce medical device management, and improve patient care (Wilson and Drozda, 2013).

Paradigm Shift: Patient Perceptions of Health and Wellness

Traditionally, people aspire to have the least healthcare issues possible so they can reduce the chances of visiting a physician or taking medication. The postmodern era created a cohort in which pleasurable lifestyles and preferred personal choices supersede disease prevention, resulting in a generation that relies on medication control with the least out-of-pocket expenses possible. Some like to use medical services more than necessary because there is a belief that insurance covers the cost. Some unethical doctors encourage patients to receive treatment that is unnecessary due to insurance coverage. Patient focus on and perceptions of healthcare services are no longer only on the treatment of a disease; a new array of augmented facilities such as quality of entertainment in a patient's room, variety of meal plans, availability of rehabilitation gardens, and process communication with patients and families account for a large portion

[9]Public Law 111–5, 123 Stat. 115, §§ 13400 et seq.

of patient satisfaction. Beginning in northern Europe, and influencing the United States, is a desire for the aging cohort to look young and stay youthful, especially in their outward appearance. Thus, a growing number of physicians are offering medical products for youthful maintenance, weight management, and others.

Demographic and socioeconomic change

A growing aged population, increased single parenthood, dual-career families, and younger diabetic and cancer patients are trends presenting much burden on our society and opportunities for the healthcare industry. Since many baby boomers live beyond their 80s, Alzheimer and genealogy are areas with growing research and new treatment needs. Single parenthood and dual-career families both have tendencies to create more opportunities for the fast food industry, which indirectly contribute to children eating more processed foods, with less parental supervision. Although there is no empirical research that suggests that single parenthood and dual-career families create more young diabetic and cancer patients, there is good reason to believe this trend is causing more parents to send their children to third-party care while they have increased career commitments. Some third-party care facilities might provide better nourishment to children than their parents, but it can also be the opposite. There is also a growing population of transsexuals and homosexuals, which potentially results in new diseases that require new treatment tools, care facilities, and medications. It is not the purpose of this book to discuss these trends and their potential influences extensively. However, healthcare administrators need to keep abreast of legislation regarding patient rights, medical ethics, and providing employee guidelines and training to avoid lawsuits.

This chapter examines industry structure and emerging models of operating health care that are more efficient and value-added to patients. Examples illustrate typical hospital structures and their characteristics. We also report on data and trends concerning labor availability, quality, and turnover, providing a glimpse into the challenges of which an executive needs to pay attention to, from strategic planning to staff management. Outside market forces such as technological and demographic changes as well as paradigm shift are also highlighted. Management issues occur in every industry, but in health care, establishing a highly committed and talented workforce is extremely challenging. Building a strong organizational culture that facilitates communication and commitment lowers turnover of essential individuals.

CHAPTER 4

Competitive Strategies

Competitive strategies are ways to make a business more successful in a market. Porter's five force analysis is a framework for industry analysis and business strategy development. It draws on industrial economics to derive forces that determine competitive intensity and therefore attractiveness of a market.[1] Discussion in this chapter elaborates on one of the five forces that bears significance on the industry in terms of ease/difficulty of entry. According to Devers, Brewster, and Casalino (2003), hospitals' strategic emphasis changed between 1996 and 1997, and 2000 and 2001. In the mid-1990s, hospitals primarily competed on price through wholesale strategies. By 2000, non-price competition gained significance and were reviving retail strategies. American hospitals now price services to various third-party payers and self-paying patients, and how the system would have to change to accommodate the increasingly popular concept of consumer-directed health care. Major factors shaping competitive strategies in health care include economic and demographic trends, regulations, public and private purchaser behaviors, and the number and type of competitors, payment methods, medical technologies, and labor supplies. Hospitals' retail strategy is to attract and retain specialists, key patients, and consumer segments. They also invest in a range of high-tech inpatient and outpatient services to attract patients (Reinhardt, 2006).

Service Differentiation

According to Lin and Wan (2001), organizational and environmental factors influence service differentiation strategies of integrated health-care networks (IHN). The tax status of an IHN, its age, and market

---

[1]Michael Lauer, "Health Care," *JAMA,* no. 13 (2006): 1659–64.

competition affect its service differentiation strategy during provision of a full continuum of care. IHNs—or integrated healthcare delivery systems—have focused heavily in the last two decades on their degree of various partnership integrations (i.e., service differentiation strategy) to offer a continuum of care. For example, Advocate Health care is a network of 13 hospitals in Illinois that cooperate to extend their range of services to provide the most effective health care. They deliver the highest-quality care for specific medical conditions over the full cycle of care by focusing on conditions that have expertise.[2] Another area that differentiates service in health care is the supply chain. Many aspects in the healthcare supply chain lead to continuously developing services. To keep up with consumption and all innovations, flexibility is essential. Complexity includes relationships, frequency of interactions, number of elements, degree of differentiation among members in the network, and the influence of supply- and customer-based complexity. With increasing customer complexities and expectations, better and more services are expected. To offer supply to complex demand, managers are working on managing and containing the complexities. With continuous growth, there needs to be adaptation to the dynamicity of the environment as increased efficiency and uncertainty preparation continues.[3]

Patient Satisfaction

Health care that improves health in a limited, technical sense (e.g., prolonging life) but does not improve the quality of life is not necessarily viewed as beneficial by patients or their families. Interest has thereby grown in not only evaluation of treatment interventions, but also the systematic assessment of care delivery. Features of patient care that influence patient satisfaction has been researched extensively in the last decade. Patient satisfaction emerged as an important indicator of a hospital's service quality, but John Hopkins research suggests it does not necessarily

[2]Michael E. Porter and Elizabeth Olmsted Teisberg, "Redefining Competition in Health Care," *Harvard Business Review* 82, no. 6 (2004): 64–76.

[3]Samyadip Chakraborty and David D. Dobrzykowski, "Supply Chain Practices for Complexity in Healthcare: A Service-Dominant Logic View," *IUP Journal of Supply Chain Management* 10, no. 3 (2013): 53–75.

reflect the quality of the surgical care patients received.[4] Dimensions that measure patient satisfaction include privacy when discussing treatment, coordination of care, physical comfort, information availability and involvement during decision making, physician availability when consultation is needed, and emotional support.[5]

Pricing Strategies

According to Winterhalter (2011), pricing is an art, and healthcare institutions should avoid charging everyone the same price. To increase profit, new services and goods alone are insufficient; adjusting pricing strategies provided to disparate customers (i.e., price discrimination) is a legitimate way of improving revenue. There are many pricing strategies from a business perspective. We focus on cost-plus pricing, value pricing, and factors that require consideration when practicing price discrimination.

Cost-Plus Pricing

Cost-plus refers to pricing a good/service by calculating a price derived from total product cost plus a profit margin that vendors prefer. It is a widely used pricing method despite some drawbacks. Cost-plus pricing does not consider competitors, consumer affordability, or fluctuating demand. Perceived value by consumers is also disregarded, resulting in a mechanical number calculated by a formula of cost plus a percentage of profit margin.

Value-Based Pricing

Value-based pricing creates a price tag that accords with the total value a product creates for a customer. It considers customers' affordability (i.e.,

---

[4]Sholom Glouberman and Henry Mintzberg, "Managing the Care of Health and the Cure of Disease—Part 1: Differentiation," *Health Care Management Review* 26, no. 1 (2001): 56–69.

[5]For details of the questionnaire, refer to C. Jenkinson et al., "Patients' Experiences and Satisfaction with Health Care: Results of a Questionnaire Study of Specific Aspects of Care," *BMJ Quality and Safety* 11, no. 4(2002): 335–39.

ability to pay) and the perceived value of a service rendered. Pricing a good/service right for varying consumer segments is challenging. Profit maximization has to take a long-term strategic view on establishing and maintaining brand equity, consumer loyalty, and market share to price value creation for disparate consumers. Some factors to consider during value-based pricing include price and availability of substitutes, consumer income, price/strength of demand for related products and services, unique characteristics/positioning relative to competitors, and overall market environment. Hospitals, willingness to provide payment plans to help patients with financing treatments is also crucial.

Insured Versus Uninsured Patients

Patients with insurance pay differently than those who have no insurance. Among insured patients, they also pay differently based on their insurance plan purchased. Prices that private health plans pay medical providers are opaque, not only to patients, but also to private purchasers.[6] When private insurers negotiate payment rates with medical providers, both parties generally agree to keep the details secret.[7] Then, the complexity of medical care contributes to pricing opaqueness. Employers—and their covered workers and dependents—pay those prices without any trace of information to the contract details negotiated on their behalf. There is no doubt that high prices lie at the heart of the health spending problem in the United States,[8] and it is equally clear that private insurers generally pay higher prices than Medicare or Medicaid.[9] Healthcare services rendered to uninsured patients might be funded by the charity

---

[6]Uwe E. Reinhardt, "The Pricing of U.S. Hospital Services: Chaos Behind a Veil of Secrecy," *Health Affairs* 25, no. 1 (January 2006).

[7]Jaime S. King, Morgan Muir, and Stephanie Alessi, "Price Transparency in the Healthcare Market," UCSF/UC *Hastings Consortium on Law, Science and Health Policy* (March 18, 2003).

[8]Gerard F. Anderson et al., "It's the Prices, Stupid: Why the United States is so Different from Other Countries," *Health Affairs* 22, no. 3 (May 2003).

[9]Stephen Zuckerman and Dana Goin, *How Much Will Medicaid Physician Fees for Primary Care Rise in 2013? Evidence from a 2012 Survey of Medicaid Physician Fees* (Menlo Park, CA: Kaiser Family Foundation, 2012), 27–33.

branch of a hospital or Medicaid. For insured patients, price variations exist both within and across states.[10]

Generally, there is little variation in primary care prices, but specialists' prices vary greatly. Prices for physician primary care services differ from hospital prices in two ways: they tend to be much closer to Medicare—and in some cases below—and they vary less within and across markets. In 13 markets studied, prices paid to primary care practices fall in a narrow range, typically between 85 and 135 percent of Medicare. Four markets—Cleveland, St. Louis, Indianapolis, and Kansas City—have wider primary care price variation, with a few primary care practices.[11]

Variation lies in negotiating leverage among providers and private insurers. Negotiating leverage is the ability to walk away if an agreement cannot be reached. In terms of negotiating leverage, primary care practices are at the bottom. Primary care physicians tend to practice solo or in smaller groups, and they are more numerous than specialists, and more substitutable. They typically have low negotiating leverage/power, and must take a price offered. A private insurer does not need the participation of all primary care physicians in a market. Instead, an insurer needs only enough primary care physicians to provide access to enrollees, and no single primary care practice is needed to reach that threshold. Therefore, few, if any, primary care practices can command prices that exceed competitors significantly.

The specialty physician market is generally more concentrated, with fewer specialist practices in each specialty than primary care physicians.[12] Specialty practices tend to be larger. Studies have found that many specialty practices have become larger in recent years to gain negotiating clout, among other reasons.[13] A patient, insured or uninsured, can expect to be charged a price

---

[10]Paul B. Ginsburg, "Wide Variation in Hospital and Physician Payment Rates Evidence of Provider Market Power," *Center for Studying Health System Change Research Brief,* no. 16 (2010).

[11]Ibid.

[12]Samuel A. Kleiner, Sean Lyons, and William D. White, "Provider Concentration in Markets for Physician Services for Patients with Traditional Medicare," *Health Management, Policy and Innovation* 1, no. 1 (September 14, 2012).

[13]Robert A. Berenson et al., "The Growing Power of Some Providers to Win Steep Payment Increases from Insurers Suggests Policy Remedies May Be Needed," *Health Affairs* 31, no. 5 (2012).

further above/below market average when receiving specialist treatment in comparison to primary care. Noteworthy is the health insurance marketplace available after enactment of the ACA. With private companies offering insurance plans from which to choose, competition will hopefully improve the price, benefits, and quality of insurance plans available to citizens.

Economies of Scale

Economies of scale refers to a proportionate saving in costs gained by increased production. In health care, it refers to the volume per given procedure as it is connected to better results.[14] It is possible by spreading the demand, which eases case programming and queue management of keen and sub-keen services.[15] Physician practices traditionally have been able to achieve modest economies of scale by sharing facilities, purchasing supplies jointly, and coordinating administrative services. Well-managed individual practice associations (IPA) can provide scaled economies through shared administrative functions, spreading risk of capitation payments, and reducing transaction costs of negotiating with hospitals and payers.[16] Horizontal integration's major objective was achieving economies of scale, which comes from large patient volumes, sharing of equipment and services, and group purchasing.[17] Accountable care organizations (ACO) suggest several ways to apply economies of scale to make health care affordable, effective, and convenient, including:

1. Application of technology to reduce the cost and time to develop protocols for evidence-based medicine and standard of care.
2. Spreading design and delivery costs of a care process over a large volume of patients, calling for more uniform processes for efficiency.

---

[14]I. Jousela et al., "Economy of Scale in Health Care Operations: Lessons from Surgical Services," *POMS 23rd Annual Conference* (2011): 1–22.

[15]Ibid.

[16]James C. Robinson and Lawrence P. Casalino, "Vertical Integration and Organizational Networks in Health Care," *Health Affairs* 15, no. 1 (1996): 7–22.

[17]Lawton R. Burns and Mark V. Pauly, "Integrated Delivery Networks: A Detour on the Road to Integrated Health Care?" *Health Affairs* 21, no. 4 (2002): 128–43.

3. Deploying technology such as cloud computing to alter fixed and variable cost structures (i.e., spread the cost of information technology over a large number of consumers).
4. Application of business model design to facilitate innovation and improvements to cost structures.[18]

Changes to contemporary health care are driven primarily by three factors:

- Systems that allows more patient care to move out of hospitals and into ambulatory settings.
- Increased regulation, making hospitals expensive to build and maintain.
- Cost shifting to patients, prompting them to empower lower-cost options for health care.

To address these changes, hospitals are building a future delivery system that will meet the outpatient-centric needs of patients in economies of scale systems.[19]

Barriers to Entry

One of Porter's five forces for evaluating the competitive landscape of an industry is barriers to entry, referring to the existence of high start-up costs or other obstacles that prevent new competitors from entering an industry or area of business easily. Obstacles can be economic, procedural, regulatory, or technological. In the case of health care, the high cost of capital, specially trained labor, and governmental permits required to construct and operate a hospital are obstacles that characterize high entry barriers. For example, the start-up, fixed costs of a hospital average over $17.5 million.[20] The University of Iowa Children's hospital that began construction in 2012 has an approximate cost of $292 million. On

[18] Accessed May 30, 2014, www.acodatabase.com/blog/economics-scale-and-accountable-care-organization-aco.

[19] Ibid.

[20] R. Roberts, "Distribution of Variable vs. Fixed Costs of Hospital Care," *JAMA* 281, no. 7 (February 7, 1999).

completion in 2016, it is expected to include 480,000 square feet in new construction and over 56,000 square feet of renovated existing space.[21]

Clinics have moderate entry barriers in comparison to hospitals. Depending on the size and scale, clinics need an approximate 25 percent of what typical hospitals require in fixed cost, which is still relatively high.[22] Clinics need some of the same technology and equipment that hospitals need. They have low variable costs in comparison to hospitals because they do not have huge inventory for consumption. Clinics are licensed by the office of statewide health and planning development. To be licensed, clinics have many standards and regulations to follow/complete. They range from sizes and accessibility of each room to the way plumbing should be installed. Limits and sizes are controlled to differentiate clinics from hospitals. Patent protection of innovated goods and service in the medical field is an area that makes the industry attractive/lucrative, but it also makes imitation of quality goods and services difficult, creating a high barrier to entry.

Corporate Strategies

Since corporate strategy refers to strategic directions organizations take to create long-term value and profit, it varies according to organizational missions, values, ownership. funding, and operational boundaries. To name a few, the ownership variety of hospitals include state-funded, university-owned, franchised, privately funded, and foundation-based. Each has a slightly different emphasis regarding mission statements and target markets, even though the general direction is the provision of healthcare services to patients and community members. They also vary in their reporting guidelines and compliance standards due to different governing requirements. Based on resources, purposes, and limitations (i.e., boundaries), hospitals formulate strategies that best serve their target markets within their scopes of expertise and locations.

[21]"UI Children's Hospital Building Update," accessed May 15, 2015, www.uichildrens.org/buildingupdate/.

[22]M. Laura Frigotto, Graziano Coller, and Paolo Collini, "The Strategy and Management Control Systems Relationship as Emerging Dynamic Process." *Journal of Management & Governance* 17, no. 3 (2013): 631–56.

Globalization

As a driver of globalization, technology influences not only commerce, but also healthcare systems. Technology enables outsourcing—contracting with another company, sometimes abroad—to have tasks performed that were previously done by the organization, or using outside suppliers and manufacturers to produce goods and services.[23] There are many reasons for outsourcing: access to a larger talent pool and operational expertise, lowering staffing/overhead costs on non-core functions, lowering risk, and so on. In health care, outsourcing diagnostic materials (e.g., x-ray) to India and having interpretation of x-ray records performed by a foreign medical professional is possible, though there is legislation underway that might soon prohibit such practices. There are strong financial incentives for hospitals to do so because it costs only a fraction of what is paid to a licensed professional in the United States. However, legal ramifications in the event of an error can be high. Whether a patient's medical records (such as an x-ray) should be handled by a hospital supplier is another question. Thus, hospitals need to be very careful in the modern world of outsourcing when "what is possible" might not be the best risk/financial option for the organization.

Another globalization-related trend in health care is medical tourism, referring to travel to another country for medical care. There is inbound (i.e., foreigners coming to your country for treatment) versus outbound (i.e., nationals going abroad to receive medical treatment). Outbound medical tourism will represent an opportunity cost to U.S. healthcare providers of $228.5 billion to $599.5 billion by 2017.[24] Keighley (2013) suggests that the U.S. Government makes policy changes to lower visa requirements to facilitate inbound medical tourism, which can bring increased revenue to the U.S. healthcare industry. Most U.S. inbound patients come from Europe, South America, the Middle East, and Canada. They seek care in the States because American providers offer some of the most advanced technologies and treatments to patients.

---

[23]Jones Gareth and Jennifer George, *Essentials of Contemporary Management* (New York: McGraw-Hill Education, 2011), 17.

[24]Keckley and Underwood "Medical Tourism: Consumers in Search of Value," Deloitte Center for Health Solutions (2008), www.deloitte.com/assets/Dcom-Croatia/Local%20Assets/Documents/hr_Medical_toudsm(3).pdf.

Strategic alliances in the healthcare industry

A strategic alliance is an agreement in which managers pool or share their organization's resources and know-how with another company (sometimes foreign), and the two organizations share the rewards and risks of starting a venture.[25] Primary benefits of strategic alliances include access to new products or markets, acquisition of technologies or skills that are too expensive or time consuming to build in-house, achieving economies of scale, spreading risk, often involving new technologies, and reducing competition.

According to Judge and Ryman (2007), a 1997 nationwide survey showed that more than two-thirds of healthcare entities were engaged in at least one strategic alliance; 33 percent of hospitals, 42 percent of managed care (payer) organizations, and 23 percent of physician group practices indicated they had joined a strategic alliance. In 2012, Walgreens and Express Scripts allied to develop a new option to refill prescriptions, pickup or direct delivery, making it easier for customers. Aramark Healthcare Technologies and Auxilio Inc. allied to offer hospitals options to manage all print-related expenses, which improves document production efficiency. Zebra Technologies and LifeMed ID Inc. announced a strategic alliance to improve patient safety and drive hospital efficiencies in 2013. With increased competition and enabling technologies, we can expect more and probably bigger strategic alliances in the years to come.

Partnerships Between the Pharmaceutical Industry and Hospitals

The pharmaceutical industry conducts research and tests, and launches new drugs in the healthcare market, to improve medical treatment/health conditions for hospitals and patients. If medical doctors in hospitals and clinics are willing to adopt a new drug, it helps with promotion and potential adoption of the new drug, creating revenue for the pharmaceutical industry. Thus, it is common for pharmaceutical companies to shower physicians with lavish meals, vacation packets, and so on to promote drug adoption. Physicians are sometimes unaware of the indirect tactics that pharmaceutical companies use to attract their attention to new drugs. What is an acceptable incentive for doctors, and when is it unethical?

[25]Gareth and George, 54.

Currently, there are no explicit guidelines on non-monetary kickbacks and what level of gifts constitutes bribery. When hospitals have good relationships with pharmaceutical companies in the form of receiving updates and knowledge on compliance issues and staff training, patient experiences improve because correct instruction on medication is available to patients, and physicians are empowered with knowledge to advise patients.[26]

Relationships Between the Insurance Industry and Hospitals

The U.S. insurance industry has unique relationships with hospitals because hospitals are paid/reimbursed based on prearranged or pre-negotiated plans. In some specialized departments, a hospital might have negotiation leverage with insurance companies on the reimbursement rate/split. In other departments, hospitals just take terms offered by an insurance company. Little is known about how these rates are derived and why. We do know, however, that in areas in which there are high insurer concentrations, hospitals are able to negotiate better payment rates.[27] After enactment of ACA, the availability of marketplace insurance plans for the public's purchase creates two immediate impact: 1) created more competition, providing more options for the uninsured population, 2) improved health insurance premiums, making it slightly more affordable for patients. This trend can hurt hospital revenue and lower margins. Such a trend can be reversed if a large portion of privately insured people enter a public plan.[28]

Relationships with Other Suppliers (e.g., Food and Medical Devices)

Each sector of health care plays a role. The catering department does not require the skill set of physicians, but is still crucial to the overall patient

---

[26]Angela Cairns and Yvonne E. Yarker, "The Role of Healthcare Communications Agencies in Maintaining Compliance When Working with the Pharmaceutical Industry and Healthcare Professionals," *Current Medical Research And Opinion* 24, no. 5 (2008): 1371–78.

[27]Erin E. Trish and Bradley J. Herring, "How Do Health Insurer Market Concentration and Bargaining Power with Hospitals Affect Health Insurance Premiums?" *Journal of Health Economics* 42 (2015): 104–14, accessed July 31, 2015.

[28]Allen Dobson et al., "How A New 'Public Plan' Could Affect Hospitals' Finances and Private Insurance Premiums," *Health Affairs (Project Hope)* 28, no. 6 (2009): 1013–24.

experience. Due to the increasing number of patients in hospitals, catering and food departments are being stretched. CEOs are cutting back on miscellaneous expenses to keep costs down.[29] With consumer pressure on healthy food and increased food cost, will the next trend be hospitals forming strategic alliance with agricultural, food, and restaurant industries? For the medical device industry, it is common for new medical instruments/devices to be lent to hospitals for a trial period to test whether the hospital should purchase them. Trial provisions influence purchasing decisions in hospitals. If implemented incorrectly, trial provisions might compromise the physical integrity, safety, and health of patients, and can lead to legal consequences for hospitals and medical staff.[30]

Relationship with Donors, Media, and Community Outreach

Creating brand name awareness of hospitals for the public is such a prevalent practice today that we see advertisements for hospitals from billboards on highways to flash boards in airport transit passages. Hospitals also staff public relations officers and donor relationship management experts to maintain good relationships with various organizations. Physicians' profiles are featured in publications, complimentary seminars showcase a hospital's expertise, and free cholesterol tests are offered to the public regularly. Progressive hospitals invest in communicating and maintaining strong relationships with donors, media, and communities.

This chapter describes the competitive landscape of the healthcare industry, with focus on hospitals. The strategic and complex relationships embedded in the healthcare system, with the backdrop of new government regulations, will steer administrators into new areas of ambiguity and ethical concerns. Although it is not the purpose of this chapter/book to discuss emergent issues, the information provided is intended to help executives prioritize long- and short-term initiatives.

[29]Tom Baum, "Food or Facilities? The Changing Role of Catering Managers in the Healthcare Environment," *Nutrition and Food Science* 36, no. 3 (2006): 138–52.
[30]P. Gonser and U. Matern, "Trial Provision in Clinical Routine: Definition of Terms and Investigation of Normal Practice," *Der Chirurg; Zeitschrift Für Alle Gebiete Der Operativen Medizen* 85, no. 1 (January, 2014): 51–56.

CHAPTER 5
Regulation

Regulations are legal requirements with which industries need to comply for meeting policy/operational standards. In health care, there are emerging rules and regulations that control medical, insurance, and pharmaceutical platforms, and others. In this chapter, a few of these regulations and acts are discussed, including their influence on the healthcare industry.

Policies that Promote/Restrict Health and Wellness/Health Care

Occupational Safety and Health Administration (OSHA) encourages employers and employees to reduce workplace hazards. Healthcare workers face a variety of health and safety risks related to chemical and drug exposures.[1] The primary threat to employees in health care is diseases that are airborne or infectious through contact. OSHA promotes health and wellness by collaborating with states that operate their own health and safety programs to establish systematic recordkeeping and reporting requirements for employers. The Family Medical Leave Act (FMLA) was established in the 1970s to offer employee job protection with unpaid leave for legitimate reason such as personal medical needs, caring for an immediate family member, military-related reasons, and others. FMLA allows workers to attend family and medical related needs without worry of job loss. As long as there is no abuse of the policy, FMLA promotes overall health and wellness by providing a safety net for job/economic stability. HIPAA is the first national regulation for the use/disclosure of an individual's

[1]U.S. Department of Safety, "Occupational Safety and Health Administration: Safety and Health Topics," accessed April 28, 2015, www.osha.gov/SLTC/healthcarefacilities/index.html.

health information. Any healthcare provider that electronically processes, stores, or transmits medical records must follow its guidelines. There are five sections of rules: security, privacy, transactions, identifiers, and enforcements.[2] In 2013, approximately one-quarter of 14,000 complaints regarding violation of HIPAA were investigated. The Act strongly restricts the healthcare industry by defining boundaries of health records used by covered entities such as healthcare clearinghouses.[3] It also forces hospitals to remain up to date.

Patient/Employee Safety

Regulations regarding patient/employee safety provide a standard of quality in which patients and employees are treated/protected. It also affects organizational reputation and overall health insurance premiums due for employers. Organizations proactive at embracing patient/employee safety might house a healthier group of employees, which provides a bargaining chip for employers when negotiating with insurance companies. OSHA requires employers to notify employees of potential hazards using color codes, posters, and training to inform employees who handle hazardous materials. It also requires employers to keep records of work-related injuries and illnesses, and provide medical examinations and access to employee medical records.

The Americans with Disabilities Act (ADA) prohibits unfair discrimination of qualified individuals with disabilities regarding the hiring, advancement, compensation, and other conditions of employment privileges. Although there are various degrees of disabilities, the ADA specifies that a disability is deemed as "a physical or mental impairment that substantially limits one or more of the major life activities of the individual."[4] HIV-infected employees are not protected by the ADA because they post a direct threat to the health and safety of other employees and patients. Thus,

---

[2]HIPAA-HITECH Guidelines, "Are You HIPAA Compliant for 2014?" accessed May 19, 2015, www.hipaaguidelines101.coms.

[3]James G. Hodge, "Health Information Privacy and Public Health," *The Journal of Law, Medicine & Ethics* 31, no. 4 (2003): 663–71.

[4]Nathan R. Wolf, "Americans with Disabilities Act," *Detroit College of Law at Michigan State University* (2000): 1–19.

HIV-infected individuals are not classified as disabled. The Food, Drug, and Cosmetic Act (1938) was passed but failed to provide control and monitoring of the production and manufacturing of food—a stage during which food can be mishandled and infected with bacteria easily. Fortunately, the healthcare industry takes serious precautions during preparation and handling of food. According to the North Carolina Department of Health and Human Services, employees are to always wash hands before and after handling food preparation for patients, and before and after patient contact, including oral feedings.[5] Employees in the healthcare industry are also mandated to separate institutional food from personal food brought from home. For instance, all food supplies from healthcare institutions in North Carolina and other states must come from sources that comply with the state's rules governing sanitation of restaurants and other food-handling establishments.

Labor Practices

According to Rossheim (2012), healthcare wages trump other industries. Construction industries' cumulative wage increases were less than 3 percent from 2006 to 2011, but healthcare workers acquired over a 9 percent increase during the same period. However, underpayment and miscalculation regarding compensation are rapidly growing issues.[6]

Wage and labor regulations

The Fair Labor Standard Act (FLSA) requires employers to maintain accurate payroll and time records, pay overtime for non-exempt employees, and establish youth employment standards that influence employees in the private sector and those in federal, state, and local governments.[7] For example, payroll

---

[5]The Department of Health and Human Services, "Rules Governing the Sanitation of Hospitals, Nursing Homes, Adult Care Homes, and Other Institutions," *North Carolina Public Health* (2012).

[6]ERS Group Economists, "Wages and Hour Claims in Health Care Industry: Trends and Analytical Responses," accessed June 3, 2015, www.ersgroup.com/whitepapers/flsa_healthcare.

[7]U.S. Department of Labor, "Compliance Assistance—Wages and the Fair Labor Standards Act (FLSA)," accessed June 3, 2015, www.dol.gov/whd/flsa.

records should be kept two to three years. Hospitals and residential care establishments can use a fixed work period of fourteen consecutive days instead of the 40-hour workweek for the purpose of computing overtime.[8]

Unions and changing trend

In the healthcare industry, unions ensure not only fair wages and compensation for their members, but also safety of medical practitioners such as physicians. In 2012, approximately 21 percent of healthcare workers were members of a union, far above the nationwide average union membership rate of 12 percent.[9] The National Labor Relations Act (NLRA) defends organizational rights and makes union efforts available to employees of healthcare institutions, but not to independent contractors; self-employed physicians who are independent contractors cannot organize collective bargaining under NLRA.

Taxation

The corporate tax of American companies is high among OECD[10] countries. Tax laws in healthcare industries are complex. A few examples that illustrate what one might need to be aware of in order to seek professional consultation are discussed later.

What is taxable and not taxable?

Medical devices are subject to an excise tax of 2.3 percent, based on sale price.[11] Washington Tax Determination#92-164, 12 WTD (1993) is an example that provides helpful tax guidelines for sales of medical instru-

---

[8]U.S. Department of Labor, "Wage and Hour Division (WHD): Fact Sheet—Wage and Hour Division (WHD)," accessed July 7, 2015, www.dol.gov/whd/.

[9]H. Punke, "How Hospitals and Unions Can Bridge Their Gaps," last modified July 3, 2003, accessed July 7, 2015, www.beckershospitalreview.com/workforce-labor-management/how-hospitals-and-unions-can-bridge-their-gaps.html.

[10]Organization for Economic Cooperation and Development (OECD).

[11]"ACA Taxes and Fees," accessed July 8, 2015, www.bcbsnc.com/assets/hcr/pdfs/spotlight_taxes_fees.pdf.

ments and supplies to hospitals. Some conclusions reached include the following:

- Surgical sutures, clips, and staples, along with disposable instruments such as staple guns, clip appliers, and loading units (i.e., cartridge devices) that apply these items to patients, are exempt from sales and use tax. Sales of nondisposable or reusable staple guns, clip appliers, and loading units are taxable. Staple removers are subject to tax, whether disposable or reusable.
- Disposable pneumoperitoneum needles are exempt from sales tax when they deliver prescribed medical gases to patients because the needles are part of the delivery system of an exempt item. If the needles are reusable on more than one patient, they are taxable as part of a hospital's surgical equipment.
- Purse string instruments, ligating loops, forceps, sizers, and trocar tips are not prosthetic or orthotic devices or ostomic items. They also do not deliver exempt items such as sutures or prescribed drugs. Thus, all are surgical instruments only, which are taxable, whether disposable.[12]

This is a very complicated subject. Suppose someone is selling a pair of glasses to a consumer. The lenses are considered prescription and are therefore not taxable, but the frames are a taxable item. This is an area in which expertise in specific location/state requirement is needed if one wants a clear picture.

Market/government intervention successes and failures

Market failure refers to the inability of a market economy to reach desirable outcomes while exploiting resources. In health care, the United States is criticized as spending twice as much as other developed countries, but is delivering bottom-tier quality healthcare services. This is one type of market failure. Governments play a role in the successes and failures of

[12]"Department of Revenue for Washington State," accessed May 18, 2015, http://dor.wa.gov/Content/Home/Default.aspx.

healthcare in a country. U.S. healthcare spending rose from 9 percent of GDP in 1980 to 16 percent in 2008; and in 2013, it accounted for 18 percent. By 2022, and considering Obamacare, healthcare spending is projected to reach $200 billion per year.[13]

Externalities

Externalities refer to the side effects or consequences of a mechanized or profitable activity that affects other parties without being reflected in the cost of the goods or services sold. For example, pollution of beaches with untreated sewage and syringes from hospitals is a negative side effect, while immunization is a positive one.[14] Welfare economics suggests that the existence of externalities results in outcomes that are not socially optimal. Those who suffer from external costs pay involuntarily, while others who enjoy external benefits do so at no cost.

If one uses the 2013 healthcare reform (Affordable Care Act [ACA]) as an example, one can list desirable and undesirable externalities that resulted external of the original plan. If an individual enrolls with Affordable Health Care, does it mean that the individual will be encouraged to visit or consult a physician before one's health problems become costly or too serious to cure? Does one enrolled with ACA have lowered healthcare spending? There are too many examples on both sides of the argument that one can find in the market. Overall, healthcare reform's objective is to provide health insurance to citizens who would otherwise be unable to afford it. Both industry practitioners and the government need to be aware of and seek to reduce, if not eliminate, externalities created from changing policies.

Opportunities and Challenges in the Healthcare Industry

Opportunities

Technological, social, and economic development in the last couple of decades has given rise to a rapid globalization movement that creates

[13]R. Avrik, "Putting Health Care Launch into Perspective," *National Review Online,* accessed July 20, 2014, http://nationalreview.com.

[14]G. Prante, "Government-Created Externalities Stemming from Intervention in Health Care Markets," *Tax Foundation,* accessed January 18, 2015, http://taxfoundation.org/.

opportunities in health care for international collaboration, medical tourism, and migrant workers.

International Collaboration

Many breakthroughs in medicine have been achieved recently among scientists who are located in different parts of the globe. For example, Dengue fever vaccine was developed. Dengue fever places about half of the world's population at risk because it was not preventable except by avoiding mosquito bites. In 2015, a new vaccine was developed and tested, and is expected to be available to treat the disease, according to WHO. Genomic medicine is also drawing international collaboration, where countries such as England, Canada, Israel, Estonia, Luxembourg, and Thailand are leading major initiatives that are expected to contribute to development of the field.[15] All of these offer benefits to the global community.

Medical Tourism

In chapter 3, medical tourism has been discussed under the globalization trend. Medical tourism refers to travel to another country to receive medical treatment. Inbound medical tourist refers to the inflow of foreigners into a country for medical treatment. Outbound medical tourist refers to the departure of a country to another for medical treatment. It is both an opportunity and a challenge for some countries. Generally, patients travel outside of their homelands for medical treatment either for better quality of care or lower bills. For Americans, Latin American countries are popular destinations for kidney transplants. Thailand is known for facial and transsexual organ surgeries. Israel is known for treatment of wounds and Sweden is known for training medical personnel with their advanced medical technologies. One way inbound medical tourism for America can be promoted is through marketing and solid collaboration between hospitals, hotels, airports, and other related after-care facilities. When foreigners travel to the States for medical treatment, all of the core tourism industries can work together to provide the

[15]National Human Genome Research Institute, "International Collaboration Aims to Speed Development of Genomic Medicine," last modified June 3, 2015, accessed January 8, 2016, https://www.genome.gov/27561782.

patients (tourists) the service they need to facilitate their medical and travel experiences. When the patient experience is positive, the word of mouth will bring back more customers to the hospitals in the States.

Migrant Workers

Workers who migrate for work are called migrant workers. An annual average of 60,000 physicians from all over the world, and nurses from Latin American and Asian countries, migrate to the U.S. healthcare system. Celebrating diversity is a human resources management priority among other development and initiatives. Other advantages that come with technological advancement include advanced research and new treatment discoveries, improved medical devices and equipment, improved quality control of medical supplies, and patient access to health records. An area that is receiving increased attention is sustainability. In health care, sustainability applies to areas such as patient safety, employee wellness, and healthcare affordability.

Challenges

Quality of care is an area that healthcare executives need to monitor to thrive in the industry. Although there are many levels of accreditation that hospitals can achieve to reach milestones at local, state, and national levels, industry accreditation is not necessarily equivalent to institutional care. The availability of technology for medical assistance has allowed so much to be performed by robots or machines that the old-day bed-side "assistance of nurses" is a fading scene in many hospitals. Patient care is performed by healthcare aids and computer-monitored machines in many nationally accredited hospitals. Patient care quality might be defined as reduced medical errors/readmittance rates by healthcare institutions, but the patient perspective of patient care can be different from a healthcare provider's.

Employee training and development in health care is a requirement for updating knowledge and skills of medical professionals. Although many welcome training opportunities, some see it as a draining exercise that takes valuable time away from work. Institutions that are strong at promoting training and development also regularly lose action staff in the field as progressive employees move into management positions. There is a strong need for strategic human resources planning to maintain a pipeline of employees for smooth operations.

Another challenge deals with atypical work hours and rampant lawsuits. Hours are usually long and changing, making the environment prone to mistakes. Insurance for medical malpractice, risk of bankruptcy, and loss of license to practice is expensive. The ACA creates opportunities for more people to be insured. However, those who are insured do not necessarily receive the level of care needed because many practitioners might not accept Obamacare plans.

Governmental restrictions, regulations, and direction

Governmental restrictions appear voluminous if one simply examines all the boundaries laid out for Medicare and Medicaid. However, every public policy, especially a societal benefit, must have guidelines and restrictions for it to be sustainable. One obvious restriction is the source of pharmaceutical products; many drugs from foreign countries may not enter the United States. Thus, some Americans try to buy foreign-made medicine/drugs online. Canada especially attracts American buyers online. Many restrictions in health care come indirectly from the combined effect of government policy stipulation and insurance policy restriction. For example, wages and benefits offered to employees in long-term care facilities are constrained by reimbursement policies, making employee retention a human resources challenge.

Since the passing of ACA, new approaches to payment reform have been underway, with the objectives of slowing spending in health care while improving the quality of care. For example, the current healthcare system rewards quantity of service rendered to patients, rather than quality of care. Bundled payments for care improvement initiatives (BPCI) are designed to test whether bundled payments align incentives for hospitals, physicians, and other healthcare providers to work closely together across many settings to achieve improved patient outcomes at lower cost.[16] The value-based purchasing program (VBP) was a pilot project in 2003, but is now mandated by the ACA, applying to over 3,200 acute-care and Medicare participating hospitals.

[16]U.S. Department of Health and Human Services, Centers for Medicare & Medicaid, Center for Medicare & Medicaid Innovation, "Bundled Payments for Care Improvement (BPCI) Initiative: General Information" (January 31, 2013), http://innovation.cms.gov/initiatives.bundledpayments/index.html.

These participating hospitals are encouraged to earn incentive payments based on clinical outcomes and patient satisfaction.[17] The program is funded by annual percentage reductions in the standard reimbursement that Medicare pays all hospitals.[18]

The ACA brought fundamental changes to U.S. health care, which are promising in the longer term, provided the focus of reform and innovation continues to be quality of patient care and disease prevention for defined populations. When all parties involved in the healthcare system strive to work concertedly instead of on disjointed, episodic treatment of patients, future health care promises to be better.

Resources for Further Study

1. Agency for Healthcare Research and Quality (www.ahrq.gov/)
2. American Medical Association (AMA)
3. British Medical Association (BMA)
4. Institute of Medicine (IOM)
5. National Center for Health Statistics (www.cdc.gov/nchs/)
6. National Library of Medicine Databases (www.nlm.nih.gov/medlineplus/)
7. Office of the National Coordinator for Health Information Technology (www.healthhit.gov/)
8. U.S. Congressional Budget Office: (http://cbo.gov)
9. U.S. Department of Health and Human Services (www.hhs.gov)
10. U.S. Food and Drug Administration (www.fda.gov)
11. World Health Organization (WHO)

---

[17] The Henry J. Kaiser Family Foundation, "Medicare Discloses Hospitals, Bonuses, Penalties Based on Quality," *Kaiser Health News* (December 20, 2012), www.kaiserhealthnews.org/stories.2012/december/21/medicare-hospitals-value-based-purchasing.aspx?p=1.

[18] U.S. Department of Health and Human Services, Centers for Medicare & Medicaid, "Frequently Asked Questions: Hospital Value-Based Purchasing Program" (March 9, 2012), www.cms.gov/Medicare/Quality-Initiatives-Patient-Assessment-Instruments/hospitals-value-based-purchasing/Downloads/FY-2013-Program-Frequently-Asked-Questions-about-Hospitals-VBP-3-9-12.pdf.

Bibliography

"2014 Health Insurance Subsidies FAQ." *eHealth.* Last modified December 23, 2013. Accessed May 28, 2014. www.ehealthinsurance.com/afforabable-care-act/news/2014-health-insurance-subsidies-faq.

"ACA Taxes and Fees." Accessed July 8, 2015. www.bcbsnc.com/assets/hcr/pdfs/spotlight_taxes_fees.pdf.

"Anesthesia." *Merriam-Webster.* Accessed March 15, 2014. www.merriam webster.com/dictionary/anesthesia.

"Department of Revenue for Washington State." Accessed May 18, 2015. http://dor.wa.gov/Content/Home/Default.aspx.

"Evergreen Healthcare Partners with API Healthcare to Get Labor Productivity and Costs Under Control." *Health & Beauty Close-Up*, March 2, 2012. http://search.proquest.com.proxy.pba.edu/docview/925655472?accountid=26397.

"Geographic Location, Services Provided, and Financial Performance." *The General Accounting Office.* Last modified October, 2003. Accessed April 28, 2014. http://gao.gov/new.items/d04167.pdf.

"Mayo Clinic History." *History of Mayo Clinic.* Accessed May 20, 2015. www.mayoclinic.org/about-mayo-clinic/history.

"OSF St. Joseph Medical Center." *osfstjoseph.org.* Accessed March 6, 2014.

"Patient Care Services: Diagnostic Services." *US Department of Veterans Affairs.* Accessed March 4, 2014. www.patientcare.va.gov/DiagnosticsServices.aspx.

"Patients and Visitors." *Baylor Health Care System.* Accessed March 4, 2014. www.baylorhealth.com/PatientVisitors/Pages?MedicalRecords.aspx.

"Public Health." *SafetyNetsFlorida.org.* Accessed April 28, 2014. safetynetsflorida.org/public.

"Services." *SelectSpecialtyHospitals.com.* Last modified April 20, 2014. Accessed April 29, 2014. www.selectspecialtyhospitals.com/services/.

"The Specialty Hospital of Washington." *Specialhospitalofwashington.com.* Accessed April 10, 2014. www.specialtyhospitalofwashington.com/types-of-patients-we-serve/.

"UI Children's Hospital Building Update." Accessed May 15, 2015. http://www.uichildrens.org/buildingupdate/.

Abelson, Reed. "The Face of Future Health Care." *The New York Times.* Last updated March 20, 2013. Accessed May 2, 2014. www.nytimes.com/2013/03/21/business/kaiser-permanente-is-seen-as-face-of-future-health-care.html?_r=0.

American Hospital Directory. "Identification and Characteristics: Ronald Reagan UCLA Medical Center." Accessed April 26, 2014. www.ahd.come/free_profile.php?-hcfa_id=a5ba61dcb726a71c1e7cb701b5b1ac1e&ek=6f44eb5cdeb9df9bd112040a543697a2.

Andrew L. Wang. "How Chicago's Top Hospitals Really Make Money." *Chicago Business*. Accessed February 3, 2014. www.chicagobusiness.com/article/20140201/-ISSUE01/302019986/how-chicagos-top-hospitals-really-make-money.

Armour, Stephanie. "Health Exchange Approved Fake Claims." *The Wall Street Journal* A3. Last updated July 16, 2015.

Avrik, R. "Putting Health Care Launch into Perspective." *National Review Online*. Accessed July 20, 2014. http://nationalreview.com.

Babb, Victoria J., and John Babb. "Pharmacist Involvement in Healthy People 2010." American Pharmaceutical Association. Last modified 2003. Accessed March 14, 2014. http://pharmacy.auburn.edu/pcs/mtms/Pharmacistinvolvementinhealthypeople2010.pdf.

Baum, Tom. "Food or Facilities? The Changing Role of Catering Managers in the Healthcare Environment." *Nutrition and Food Science* 36, no. 3 (2006): 138–52.

Beecher, Henry K., and Donald P. Todd. "A Study of the Deaths Associated with Anesthesia and Surgery: Based on a Study of 599,548 Anesthesias in Ten Institutions 1948–1952, Inclusive." *Annals of Surgery* 140, no. 1 (1954).

Belok, David. "The True Cost of Healthcare." Accessed December 15, 2011. http://truecostofhealthcare.org/outpatient_charges/diagnostic_tests.

Berenson, Robert A. et al. "The Growing Power of Some Providers to Win Steep Payment Increases from Insurers Suggests Policy Remedies may be Needed." *Health Affairs* 31, no. 5 (2012).

Black, Henry C. *The Law Dictionary*. 2nd ed. Clark, NJ: The Lawbook Exchange, 1995.

Bureau of Labor Statistics. "Economic News Release." Last modified December 9, 2015. Accessed June 10, 2015, www.bls.gov/news.release/ecec.nr0.htm.

Burns, Lawton R., and Mark V. Pauly. "Integrated Delivery Networks: A Detour on the Road to Integrated Health Care?" *Health Affairs* 21, no. 4 (2002).

Cairns, Angela, and Yvonne E. Yarker. "The Role of Healthcare Communications Agencies in Maintaining Compliance When Working With the Pharmaceutical Industry and Healthcare Professionals." *Current Medical Research and Opinion* 24, no. 5 (2008): 1371–78.

Chakraborty, Samyadip, and David D. Dobrzykowski. "Supply Chain Practices for Complexity in Healthcare: A Service-Dominant Logic View." *IUP Journal of Supply Chain Management* 10, no. 3 (2013).

Cleverley, Williams O., and Paula H. Song. *Essentials of Health Care Finance*. 7th ed. Sudbury, MA: Jones & Bartlett Learning, 2011.

Cliff, Sarah, and Dan Keating. "One Hospital Charges $8,000—Another, $38,000." *Washington Post*. Last updated May 8, 2013. Accessed April 29, 2014. www.washingtonpost.com/blogs/wonkblog/wp/2013/05/08/one-hospital-8000-another-38000/.

Commodity Exchange Act, U.S. Code 18 (1961), §§ 1956–1957.

Commodity Exchange Act, U.S. Code 31, §§ 3729 et seq.

Conroy, Joanne, Michael Weitekamp, Meaghan Quinn, Tom Enders, Molly Smith, Carl Mankowitz, Lynn Chafetz, and Brian Owners. "Virginia Mason Medical Center: Applying LEAN Methodology to Lead Quality and Transform Health." *AAMC Readiness for Reform* (2011).

Cutler, David M. "From the Affordable Care Act to Affordable Care." *JAMA: Journal of the American Medical Association* 314, no. 4 (2015): 337–38. doi:10.1001/jama.2015.7683. http://search.proquest.com.proxy.pba.edu/docview/1719428242?accountid=26397.

Davis, Lisa A. "Acute Care Hospital Expenses for FY 2011." Connecticut Department of Public Health. Last modified February 2013. Accessed March 14, 2014. www.ct.gov/dph/lib/dph/ohca/publications/2013/2011_expense_fact_sheet.pdf.

Devers, Kelly J., Linda R. Brewster, and Lawrence P. Casalino, "Changes in Hospitals Competitive Strategy: A New Medical Arms Race?" *Health Services Research* 38, no. 1 (2003): 447–69, p. 2.

Dlugacz, Yosef D. *Value-Based Health Care: Linking Finance and Quality*. San Francisco: Jossey-Bass Publishing, 2010.

Dobson, Allen, Joan E. DaVanzo, Audrey M. El-Gamil, and Gregory Berger. "How a New 'Public Plan' Could Affect Hospitals' Finances and Private Insurance Premiums." *Health Affairs (Project Hope)* 28, no. 6 (2009): 1013–24.

Environmental Protection Agency. "Guidelines for the Management of Biomedical Waste in the Northwest Territories." Accessed May 28, 2014. http://www.enr.gov.nt.ca/sites/dafult/files/guidelines/biomedical_waste.pdf.

ERS Group Economists. "Wages and Hour Claims in Health Care Industry: Trends and Analytical Responses." Accessed June 3, 2015. http://www.ersgroup.com/whitepapers/flsa_healthcare.

FAQS. "Baylor University Medical Center in Dallas, Texas (TX)." Accessed April 27, 2014. www.faqs.org/tax-exempt/TX/Baylor-University-Medical-Center.html.

Forrest, Christopher B., Paul A. Nutting, Sarah von Schrader, Charles Rhode, and Barbara Starfield. "Primary Care Physician Specialty Referral Decision Making: Patient, Physician, and Health Care System Determinants." John Hopkins University. Last modified September 09, 2010. Accessed May 18, 2014. www.jhsph.edu/research/centers-and-institutes/johns-hopkins-primary-carae-policy-center/Publications_PDFs/A216.pdf.

Frigotto, M. Laura, Graziano Coller, and Paolo Collini. "The Strategy and Management Control Systems Relationship as Emerging Dynamic Process." *Journal of Management & Governance* 17, no. 3 (2013): 631–56.

Galewitz, Phillip. "Medicaid Helps Hospitals Pay for Illegal Immigrants' Care." Last modified February 12, 2013. Accessed April 28, 2014. http://khn.org/news/medicaid-illegal-immigrant-emergency-care/.

Garahani, M. L. "Educational Practices Accomplished by Hospital Nurses Published in National Journals." *Ciencia* (2009).

Gareth, Jones, and Jennifer George. *Essentials of Contemporary Management.* New York: McGraw-Hill Education, 2011.

Gerard F. Anderson et al., "It's the Prices, Stupid: Why the United States is so Different from Other Countries." *Health Affairs* 22, no. 3 (May 2003).

Ginsburg, Paul B. "Wide Variation in Hospital and Physician Payment Rates Evidence of Provider Market Power." *Center for Studying Health System Change Research Brief,* no. 16 (2010): 1–11.

Glouberman, Sholom, and Henry Mintzberg. "Managing the Care of Health and the Cure of Disease—Part 1: Differentiation." *Health Care Management Review* 26, no. 1 (2001).

Gonser, P., and U. Matern. "Trial Provision in Clinical Routine: Definition of Terms and Investigation of Normal Practice." *Der Chirurg; Zeitschrift Für Alle Gebiete Der Operativen Medizen* 85, no. 1 (January 2014): 51–56.

Gostin, Lawrence O., Peter D. Jacobson, Katherine L. Record, and Lorian E. Hardcastle. "Restoring Health to Health Reform: Integrating Medicine and Public Health to Advance the Population's Well-Being." *University of Pennsylvania Law Review* 159, no. 6 (2011): 1777–1823.

Hall XII. "Survey of Recent Developments in Health Care Law." *Health Law* (2011).

HIPAA-HITECH Guidelines. "Are You HIPAA Compliant for 2014?" Accessed May 19, 2015. www.hipaaguidelines101.coms.

Hodge, James G. "Health Information Privacy and Public Health." *The Journal of Law, Medicine & Ethics* 31, no. 4 (2003).

Howle, Elaine M. "UCLA and UCSF Medical Centers." *California State Auditor,* 2014.

Hutchinson, Reed. "CFO Explains Hospital's Finance to Employees." *UCLA Today: Faculty and Staff News.* Accessed April 28, 2014. www.today.ucla.edu/portal/ut/PRN-050816people_cfo.aspx.

Iglehart, John. "Vision for Change in the U.S. Healthcare." *New England Journal of Medicine* (2009).

Jenkinson, C., A. Coulter, S. Bruster, N. Richards, and T. Chandola. "Patients' Experiences and Satisfaction with Health Care: Results of a Questionnaire Study of Specific Aspects of Care." *BMJ: Quality and Safety,* no. 4 (2002).

Jost, Timothy. "An Affordable Care Act at Year 5: Key Issues for Improvement." *JAMA* 313, no. 17 (May 5, 2015): 1709–10.

Jousela, I., M. Lepantalo, A. Peltokorpi, and P. Torkki. "Economy of Scale in Health Care Operations: Lessons from Surgical Services." In *POMS 23rd Annual Conference, 2011.*

Judge, William Q., and Joel A. Ryman. "The Shared Leadership Challenge in Strategic Alliances: Lessons from the U.S. Healthcare Industry." *Academy of Management Executive* 15, no. 2 (2001): 71–79.

Kaufman, Hall & Associates, Inc. *A Guide to Financing Strategies for Hospitals With Special Consideration for Smaller Hospitals*. Chicago: Kaufman, Hall & Associates, Inc., 2010.

Keckley, Paul H., and Underwood, Howard R. "Medical Tourism: Consumers in Search Of Value." Deloitte Center for Health Solutions (2008). http://www.deloitte.com/assets/Dcom-Croatia/Local%20Assets/Documents/hr_Medical_toudsm(3).pdf.

Keighley, T. "Globalization: Grasping the Concept Within the Context of Nursing". *International Nursing Review* (2013): 86.

King, Jaime S., Morgan Muir, and Stephanie Alessi. "Price Transparency in the Healthcare Market." *UCSF/UC Hastings Consortium on Law, Science and Health Policy*, March 18, 2003.

Kleiner, Samuel A., Sean Lyons, and William D. White. "Provider Concentration in Markets for Physician Services for Patients with Traditional Medicare." *Health Management, Policy and Innovation* 1, no. 1 (September 14, 2012).

Kolowitz, Brian, Gonzalo Lauro, Charles Barkey, Harry Black, Karen Light, and Christopher Deible. "Workflow Continuity—Moving Beyond Business Continuity in a Multisite 24-7 Healthcare Organization." *Journal of Digital Imaging* 25, no. 6 (2012): 744–50.

Langabeer II, J. R., and Helton, J. "Health Care Operations Management: A System Perspective". 2nd ed. Burlington, MA: Jones and Bartlett Learning, 2014.

Lauer, Michael. "Health Care." *JAMA*, no. 13 (2006): 1659–64.

Lin, Yen Ju, and Thomas T. H. Wan. "Effect of Organizational and Environmental Factors on Service Differentiation Strategy of Integrated Healthcare Network." *Health Services Management Research* 14, no. 1 (2001): 18–26.

Lunenberg, Fred C. "Human Resource Planning: Forecasting Demand and Supply." *International Journal of Management Business, and Administration* 15, no. 1 (2012).

Madeleine Estryn-Behar. "Longitudinal Analysis of Personal and Work-Related Factors Associated with Turnover Among Nurses." *Nursing Research* (2010).

Margolis, Charles. "Virginia Mason Medical Center's New 30-yr Taxable Bond." *Learn Bonds.* Last updated 2013. Accessed April 26, 2014. www.learnbonds.com/-virginia-mason-medical-centers-news-30-year-taxable-bonds.

McDonald, Kevin. "Why Privatization is not Enough." *Harvard Business Review*, May–June 1993.

Morrissey, John. "Before They Were Famous: Sentara's Bernd Started Thinking About EHRs As Far Back As 1992." *Modern Healthcare* 40, no. 24 (June 14, 2010).

National Human Genome Research Institute. "International Collaboration Aims to Speed Development of Genomic Medicine." Last modified June 3, 2015. Accessed January 8, 2016. www.genome.gov/27561782.

Needham, Brian R. "The Truth About Patient Experience: What We Can Learn from Other Industries, and How Three Ps Can Improve Health Outcomes, Strengthen Brands, and Delight Customers." *Journal of Healthcare Management* 57, no. 4 (2012): 255–63.

Nowicki, Michael. *The Financial Management of Hospitals and Healthcare Organizations*, 267. Chicago: Health Administration Press, 2004.

OECD. "Economic Survey of the United States 2008: Health Care Reform." Accessed May 22, 2014. December 9, 2008. www.keepeek.com/Digital-Asset-Management/oecd/economics/oecd-economic-surveys-united-states-2008_eco_surveys-usa-2008-en#page1.

Owens, Andrew. "Mayo Merger." *PostBulletin.com*. Last modified July 28, 2011. Accessed April 28, 2014. www.postbulletin.com/news/local/mayo-merger-mayo-clinic-s-governing-structure-has-evolved-since/article_736f464f-0fee-5741-9fc0-31e197ba1990.html.

Page, Leigh. "50 Integrated Delivery Systems to Know." *Beckers Hospital Review*. Last modified October 14, 2010. Accessed March 12, 2014. www.beckershospital-review.com/hospital-physician-relationships/50-integrated-delivery-system-to-know.html.

Porter Michael E., and Thomas H. Lee. "The Strategy That Will Fix Healthcare." *Harvard Business Review*, October 2013.

Porter, Michael E., and Elizabeth Olmsted Teisberg. "Redefining Competition in Health Care." *Harvard Business Review* 82, no. 6 (2004).

Prante, G. "Government-Created Externalities Stemming from Intervention in Health Care Markets." *Tax Foundation*. Accessed January 18, 2015. http://taxfoundation.org/.

Punke, H. "How Hospitals and Unions Can Bridge Their Gaps." Last modified July 3, 2003. Accessed July 7, 2015. www.beckershospitalreview.com/workforce-labor-management/how-hospitals-and-unions-can-bridge-their-gaps.html.

Radnofsky, Louise, and Stephanie Armour. "Medicare Plans Fixed Rate on Knee, Hip Replacements." *Wall Street Journal* A4 (July 10, 2015).

Reinhardt, Uwe E. "The Pricing of U.S. Hospital Services: Chaos Behind a Veil of Secrecy." *Health Affairs* 25, no. 1 (January 2006).

Riemschneider, Bea. "The Next-Generation Pharmacist: What Will the Future Look Like for Pharmacy?" *Pharmacy Times*. Last modified September 28, 2010. Accessed March 14, 2014. www.pharmacytimes.com/publications/issue/2010/September2010/NGP_Future_of_Pharmacy-0910.

Roberts, R. "Distribution of Variable vs. Fixed Costs of Hospital Care." *JAMA* 281, no. 7 (February 7, 1999).

Robinson, James C., and Lawrence P. Casalino. "Vertical Integration and Organizational Networks in Health Care." *Health Affairs* 15, no. 1 (1996).

Rossheum, J. "Recruiting and Hiring Advice." In the News: *Health Care Wages Trumps Other Industries*, April 25, 2012. Accessed May 25, 2015. http://hiring.monster.com/hr/hr-best-practices/recruiting=hiring=advice/healthcare-news/healthcare-wages.aspx.

Senger, Alyene. "Obamacare's Impact on Today's and Tomorrow's Taxpayers." Last modified August 21, 2013. Accessed May 25, 2014.http://www.heritage.org/research/re-ports/2013/08/obamacares-impact-on-todays-and-tomorrows-taxpayers-an-update.

Stanton, Mark. "Hospital Nurse Staffing and Quality of Care." *Research in Action*, no. 14 (March, 2004).

Sultz, Harry A., and Kristina M. Young. *Health Care USA: Understanding Its Organization and Delivery*. Burling, MA: Jones and Bartlett Learning, 2014.

The Department of Health and Human Services. "Rules Governing the Sanitation of Hospitals, Nursing Homes, Adult Care Homes, and Other Institutions." *North Carolina Public Health* (2012).

Toussaint, John. "Writing the New Playbook for U.S. Health Care: Lessons from Wisconsin Health Affairs." *Health Affairs* 28, no. 5 (2009): 1343–50.

Trish, Erin E., and Bradley J. Herring. "How Do Health Insurer Market Concentration and Bargaining Power with Hospitals Affect Health Insurance Premiums?" *Journal of Health Economics* 42 (2015): 104–14. Accessed July 31, 2015.

Tynan, Ann, "General Hospitals, Specialty Hospitals and Financially Vulnerable Patients." *HSChange.com*. Last modified April 10, 2014. Accessed April 30, 2014. www.hschange.com/CONTENT/1056/.

U.S. Department of Labor. "Compliance Assistance-Wages and the Fair Labor Standards Act (FLSA)." Accessed June 3, 2015. http:// www.dol.gov/whd/flsa.

U.S. Department of Labor. "Wage and Hour Division (WHD): Fact Sheet—Wage and Hour Division (WHD)." Accessed July 7, 2015. http://www.dol.gov/whd/.

U.S. Department of Safety. "Occupational Safety and Health Administration: Safety and Health Topics." Accessed April 28, 2015. www.osha.gov/SLTC/healthcarefacilities/index.html.

UCLA Health. "Ronald Reagan UCLA Medical Center." Accessed March 10, 2014. www.uclahealth.org/body_med.cfm?=903.

United States Department of Labor. "Fastest Growing Occupations, 2014–24." Last modified December 19, 2013. Accessed July 1, 2015. www.bls.gov/news.release/ecopro.t05.htm.

United States Department of Labor. "Health Care." *Spotlight on Statistics*. Last modified November, 2009. Accessed July 5, 2015. www.bls.gov/spotlight/2009/health_care/.

United States Department of Labor. "Occupational Employment and Wages in Cape Coral-Fort Myers—May 2014." Accessed June 30, 2015. http://www.bls.gov/regions/south-east/newsrelease/occupationalemploymentandwages_capecoral.htm.

United States v. Kats, 871 F.2d 105 (9th Cir. 1989).

West, Collin P., and Denise M. Dupras. "General Medicine vs Subspecialty Career Plans Among Internal Medicine Residents." *JAMA* 308, no. 21 (December 5, 2012): 2241–47.

Wilson, N. A., and Drozda, J. "Value of Unique Device Identification in the Digital Health Infrastructure." *JAMA* 309, no. 20 (2013): 2107–08. doi:10.1001/jama.2013.5514.

Winterhalter, Sandra J. "Economic Factors Converge: Force Hospitals to Review Pricing Strategies." *Journal of Health Care Finance* 37, no. 4 (2011): 15–35.

Wolf, Nathan R. "Americans with Disabilities Act." *Detroit College of Law at Michigan State University* (2000).

Yeigan, Jill, and Dolores Yanagihara. "Value-Based Pay for Performance: Rewarding Affordability Alongside Quality." *Health Affairs Blog*. Last updated January 14, 2014. Accessed March 20, 2014. http://healthaffairs.org/blog/2014/01/14/value-based-pay-for-performance-rewarding-affordability-alongside-quality/.

Zuckerman, Stephen, and Dana Goin. *How Much Will Medicaid Physician Fees for Primary Care Rise in 2013? Evidence from a 2012 Survey of Medicaid Physician Fees*. Menlo Park, CA: Kaiser Family Foundation, 2012.

Related Books and Articles

Abramson, John. *Overdosed America: The Broken Promise of American Medicine.* New York: HarperCollins Publisher, 2006.

Cutler, David M. "From the Affordable Care Act to Affordable Care." *JAMA: Journal of the American Medical Association* 314, no. 4 (2015): 337–38. doi:10.1001/jama.2015.7683. http://search.proquest.com.proxy.pba.edu/docview/1719428242?accountid=26397

Devers, Kelly J., Linda R. Brewster, and Lawrence P. Casalino. "Changes in Hospitals Competitive Strategy: A New Medical Arms Race?" *Health Services Research* 38, no. 1, p. 2 (2003): 447–69.

Judge, William Q., and Joel A. Ryman. "The Shared Leadership Challenge in Strategic Alliances: Lessons from the U.S. Healthcare Industry." *Academy of Management Executive* 15, no. 2 (2001): 71–79.

Keighley, T. "Globalization: Grasping the Concept Within the Context of Nursing". *International Nursing Review* (2013): 86.

Langabeer II, J. R., and J. Helton. "Health Care Operations Management: A System Perspective". 2nd ed. Burlington, MA: Jones and Bartlett Learning, 2014.

Lin, Yen Ju, and Thomas T. H. Wan. "Effect of Organizational and Environmental Factors on Service Differentiation Strategy of Integrated Healthcare Network." *Health Services Management Research* 14, no. 1 (2001): 18–26.

Porter, Michael, and Elizabeth Teisberg. *Redefining Health Care: Creating Value-Based Competition on Results. Boston:* Harvard Business Press, 2006.

Reinhardt, Uwe E. "The Pricing of US Hospital Services: Chaos Behind a Veil of Secrecy." *Health Affairs* 25, no. 1 (2006): 57–69.

Rossheum, J. "Recruiting and Hiring Advice." In the News: *Health Care Wages Trumps Other Industries,* April 25, 2012. Accessed May 25, 2015. http://hiring.monster.com/hr/hr-best-practices/recruiting=hiring=advice/healthcare-news/healthcare-wages.aspx.

Studer, Quint. *Hardwiring Excellence.* Gulf Breeze, FL: Fire Starter Publishing, 2003.

Sultz, Harry A., and Kristina M. Young. "Health Care USA: Understanding Its Organization and Delivery." Burlington, MA: Jones and Bartlett Learning, 2014.

Wilson, N. A., and J. Drozda. "Value of Unique Device Identification in the Digital Health Infrastructure." *JAMA: Journal of the American Medical Association* 309, no. 20 (2013): 2107–08. doi:10.1001/jama.2013.5514.

Winterhalter, Sandra J. "Economic Factors Converge: Force Hospitals to Review Pricing Strategies." *Journal of Health Care Finance* 37, no. 4 (2011): 15–35.

Zuckerman, Alan. "Health Care Strategic Planning." Foundation of the American Health Care Executives. *Medscape.com,* 2012.

Index

OTHER TITLES IN OUR INDUSTRY PROFILES COLLECTION

Donald Stengel, California State University, Fresno, *Editor*

- *A Profile of the Automobile and Motor Vehicle Industry: Innovation, Transformation, Globalization* by James M. Rubenstein
- *A Profile of the Software Industry: Emergence, Ascendance, Risks, and Rewards* by Sandra A. Slaughter
- *A Profile of the Performing Arts Industry: Culture and Commerce* by David H. Gaylin
- *A Profile of the Hospitality Industry* by Betsy Bender Stringam and Charles Partlow
- *A Profile of the Global Airline Industry* by Kent Gourdin
- *A Profile of the Steel Industry: Global Reinvention for a New Economy, Second Edition* by Peter Warrian
- *Company and Industry Research: Strategies and Resources* by Hiromi Kubo and Thomas J. Ottaviano

Business Expert Press has over 30 collection in business subjects such as finance, marketing strategy, sustainability, public relations, economics, accounting, corporate communications, and many others. For more information about all our collections, please visit www.businessexpertpress.com/collections.

Business Expert Press is actively seeking collection editors as well as authors. For more information about becoming an BEP author or collection editor, please visit www .businessexpertpress.com/author

Announcing the Business Expert Press Digital Library

Concise e-books business students need for classroom and research

This book can also be purchased in an e-book collection by your library as

- a one-time purchase,
- that is owned forever,
- allows for simultaneous readers,
- has no restrictions on printing, and
- can be downloaded as PDFs from within the library community.

Our digital library collections are a great solution to beat the rising cost of textbooks. E-books can be loaded into their course management systems or onto student's e-book readers.

The **Business Expert Press** digital libraries are very affordable, with no obligation to buy in future years. For more information, please visit **www.businessexpertpress.com/librarians.** To set up a trial in the United States, please contact **sales@businessexpertpress.com.**

www.ingramcontent.com/pod-product-compliance
Lightning Source LLC
Chambersburg PA
CBHW071505200326
41519CB00019B/5875

* 9 7 8 1 6 0 6 4 9 9 8 2 5 *